The Islands of Canada

Marian Engel & J.A.Kraulis

The Islands of Canada

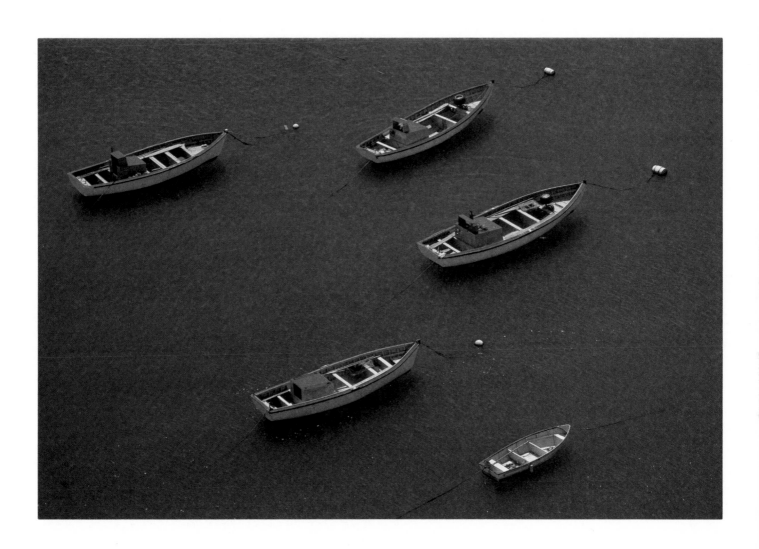

Hurtig Publishers
Edmonton

Hurtig Publishers Ltd.
10560–105 Street
Edmonton, Alberta

Canadian Cataloguing in Publication Data

Engel, Marian, 1933–
    The islands of Canada

    Includes index.
    ISBN 0-88830-203-7

    1. Islands — Canada. 2. Canada — Description
and travel — 1950-   — Views.*   3. Islands.
I. Kraulis, J. A., 1949–   II. Title.
FC75.E53   917.1   C81-091186-8
F1016.E53

Printed and bound in Canada

Contents

Introduction / 11
Acknowledgements / 13
The Queen Charlotte Islands / 17
The Inside Passage / 21
The Gulf Islands / 22
The Islands of the Great Lakes / 25
St. Joseph Island / 26
Manitoulin and the Islands of Georgian Bay / 28
The Fishing Islands / 30
Pelee Island / 31
The Toronto Islands / 33
The Thousand Islands / 34
Montréal and Surrounding Islands / 35
Île d'Orléans / 37
Grosse Île/Île de la Quarantaine / 38
Île aux Coudres / 39
Anticosti Island / 40
Prince Edward Island / 42
The Magdalen Islands/Îles de la Madeleine / 45
Nova Scotian Islands / 47
Cape Breton Island / 48
Île de la Demoiselle / 49
Island Bird Sanctuaries / 50
Fogo Island / 51
Newfoundland / 54
The Call of the Islands / 56

Page One: Like a covering of emerald velvet, sea alga decks a rock shelf on Brier Island, Nova Scotia.

Page Two: Gulls line up to see what the next wave will bring on Chesterman Beach, Vancouver Island.

Page Three: Fishing skiffs and a dory contribute an outport flavour to the harbour at St. John's, Newfoundland.

Page Four: A weathered, garlanded stairway provides access to a small, secluded beach on Pender Island, British Columbia.

Above: Golden sugar maples flank the P-line road on St. Joseph Island in Lake Huron.

Opposite: Diffused in this twilight time exposure, winter waves sweep the rocky shore of Brier Island at the entrance to the Bay of Fundy.

For Charlotte Engel
whose idea it was

Marian Engel

For Linda

J. A. Kraulis

Overleaf Verso: Surrounded by cliffs and
sensational surf, gannets take a break from
fishing at Cape St. Mary's, Newfoundland.

Overleaf Recto: Treeless Baffin Island supports
abundant wildlife, including this curious
arctic hare who came to investigate the
photographer's camp, feigning indifference.

Introduction

Somewhere among the notebooks of Gideon I once found a list of diseases as yet unclassified by medical science, and among these there occurred the word Islomania, *which was described as a rare but by no means unknown affliction of spirit. There are people, Gideon used to say, by way of explanation, who find islands somehow irresist-ible. The mere knowledge that they are on an island, a little world surrounded by the sea, fills them with an indescribable intoxication. These born "islomanes," he used to add, are the direct descendants of the Atlanteans, and it is towards the lost Atlantis that their subconscious yearns throughout their island life.*

Lawrence Durrell
Reflections on a Marine Venus

I should like to have met Gideon, for I also am afflicted with islomania, though there is nothing Atlantean in my earthly origins. And the islands I am writing about here are equally unafflicted by European cultural history: there are no shrines on them to Artemis and Aphrodite, few churches dedicated to later cognates of the Marine Venus. Where they are spirit-haunted, they echo with the laughter of Stone Age gods, the animistic spirits who clothe themselves in the garments of Raven and Eagle and Snake and Whale and Bear. Where they are history-haunted, they connect us not with Ulysses but with the stone seaports of both sides of the English Channel, or with Portugal and Spain.

Canadian islands, even as skeletal apparitions on maps, have their own savour, their own appealing abandon. Part of their romance is their true isolation, the fact that some are for long periods untouched by human hand and foot. For the rest, we seek out islands for our own reasons.

These reasons run deep in all of us. We grew up on island stories like *The Tempest, Robinson Crusoe, Treasure Island*, and many of us came to Canada from island cultures: Britain and Ireland, Sicily and Greece, and Brittany and the Île de France (which think and feel like islands).

Canada is comically rich in islands. We speak casually of them in thousands. The Arctic is almost completely composed of islands (though they are often connected by treacherous pack ice) and Baffin is one of the largest islands in the world. Two of our provinces are islands, while Cape Breton and Vancouver Island have their own separateness: one feels they ought to be provinces. There are hundreds of thousands of lakes, each of which has its islands. Is there a Canadian who has not, travelling in summer, found his own island?

It is ridiculous to attempt to document them all. Instead, Janis Kraulis and I have travelled to those that we thought were important or that we simply loved, attempting each in our own way to put down some of the magic that is available there to islomanes.

I have, in many cases, explored their history, because the islands are the oldest and most used parts of Canada. You have to close your eyes and wish yourself back a couple of centuries — or sometimes only fifty years — to understand this.

Opposite: Owned by Ivan and Brunie Naus of Pender Island, British Columbia, this goat provides abundant milk and asks for little in return, feeding on forest underbrush much of the time.

Before there were airplanes and trains and buses, all approaches to Canada were by water, and most first stops were islands. It was not by accident that Newfoundland was the first part of North America settled, that the first furniture makers in Québec plied their trade on Île aux Coudres, that Montréal was an island city. Indian wars were often conducted from islands, and fortified islands within and without the Great Lakes were the basis of some of the great fur-trading empires.

Islands in their nothingness are everything to us, the heart of our history and the home of the imagination. They remain, in Canada, extraordinarily difficult to live on; and because of various projects — particularly education — which require centralization to improve standards, many of them have been relegated to the hall-closet roles of Indian reserve, summer resort, and artists' colony. Since artists above all need the silence of islands to hear themselves think, a disproportionate number of them can be found on Canadian islands, though you often also meet them on city streets, trying desperately to load up with supplies and intellectual stimulation.

You can go crazy on islands, lured by the seal sirens who dominate your self-constructed world. You can get sane on islands, away from the distraction of city life. Above all, you can dream of and about them. We hope this book will assist you in that project. If your favourite island isn't in it, be consoled: it's still a secret.

Marian Engel
Toronto, 1981

Acknowledgements

I am indebted to many more people than I can name, but particularly to Bob Brandeis and the staff of the library at Victoria University, Toronto; the University of Toronto Press; Jane Rule, Helen Sonthoff, and Mary Johns on Galiano Island; Sara Stambaugh; Mercedes Ryan of Fogo; Farley and Claire Mowat; Kay Punch and Hugh Macmillan; Libby Oughton, Marlene Stanton, Reshard Gool, Hilda Woolnough, and Grace Taylor of P.E.I.; and Marjorie Whitelaw of Halifax. Zara Abdy of Edmonton helped with the research. The quotation from Lawrence Durrell's *Reflections on a Marine Venus* is printed with permission from Messrs. Faber and Faber, London, England.

Marian Engel

Without the generous assistance and warm hospitality of people whose islands I visited, my task would have been much more difficult and this book would have been considerably poorer. I am grateful to many people, but I must thank in particular Alfie Collinson, the Lightbown household and especially Sherri Lightbown and Sunni Beynon, Claude and Sarah Davidson, Florence Davidson, Gary and Jennie Edenshaw, Beatrice Brown, Harold Yeltatzie and Maureen Brown, Thom Henley, David Phillips, Victor Adams, Sharon Hitchcock, Bo Curtis and Cathy Young, Allan and Darlene Tansky, Steve and Fran Morrow and Dennis Seidemann, Ross Fuoco, Dr. David Usher and Sharon Lazare, Wayne and Anne Ngan, Frances Martini, Carol and Richard Martin, Maria Watson, Horst and Joyce Klein, Bob and Marjorie Russell, Ivan and Brunie Naus, Neptune and Dorothy Grimmer, Gregory and Shay Foster, Elizabeth Hopkins, Alan and Hazel Steward, Tom Toybee, Richard and Anne Royal, John Piatt, Pat Ryan, Herb Leavitt, Russell Cook and Stephen Green, Elmer F. Holl and Phil and Pat Parish.

I also wish to thank Mel Hurtig, David Shaw, Pat Morrow, Dr. Nick Drager, Rita and Dzidris Silins, Linda Küttis, and my parents.

J. A. Kraulis

Page 14, Upper: With the profile of Saltspring Island behind, a sailboat cruises the busy waters among the Gulf Islands of British Columbia.

Page 14, Lower: Fishing floats and lines add their brilliant hues to the colour of Clark's Harbour on Cape Sable Island, Nova Scotia.

Page 15: Fish nets piled along the waterfront at Tiverton on Long Island, Nova Scotia.

The Queen Charlotte Islands

This island group lies off the Pacific coast about 250 kilometres north of Vancouver Island. There are two main islands, Graham and Moresby, and some hundred and fifty smaller ones. Major centres are Queen Charlotte City, Sandspit, and Port Clements. The Queen Charlottes are the ancient home of the Haida people, and the first European to discover them was reputedly the Spanish explorer Juan Pérez, in 1774.

There is an aura of magic about the Queen Charlotte Islands, but it is hard to discover quite how that is generated. Charlotte lovers give you the impression that the islands disappear every evening at sunset and reappear every morning, renewed in the splendour of Haida myth, towed by Raven, choired by eagles, and crowned with silver and argillite. In fact, they are isolated, desolate, and, like all real places, a combination of sordidness and beauty which appeals to some people and irritates others. Now that a new car ferry has been instituted to increase tourism, a good many of the residents fear being overrun by travellers. Getting around the Charlottes by road remains, however, a difficult enough sport to ward off the less-than-stalwart. Perhaps the residents don't have to worry.

Lumber camps, iron mines, crab canneries, and peat moss plants have made work available, but it is well to remember that there is little arable (or even buildable-on) land on this rough terrain, that few sites had electricity and many roads were still planked in the 1950s. The kind of people who live in the Charlottes are not suburbanites: this is survival country. The city person who goes to rough it in the bush has often been a community liability.

Sandspit, the small town on Moresby Island, contains the airport, a few stores, not much else. To get to Graham Island and the larger communities, you drive or take the bus to Alliford Sound and cross the inlet to Skidegate. This is an arm of the open Pacific and has been described — particularly by Emily Carr, who came up here to paint — as wild and difficult. On the day I crossed, it was as blue and as magical as the fiords of Norway; but there were no stave churches and no great power lines along the shores as there are in Norway. This is wild country, no longer dominated by the totem poles that Emily, clutching her griffon dog and paint box in an open boat, came to paint. There is so little left of Haida civilization along the inlet and the Sound that it is possible to believe that you are the first person to penetrate this wilderness.

Typically for the Charlottes, there are two towns on the north side of the inlet, the Indian Skidegate, with its mission and new longhouse, and Queen Charlotte City, a fishing village considerably enlivened by a new generation of back-to-the-landers, who cover their odd-shaped and improvised houses (clinging to the edge of the land below Slatechuck Mountain) with cedar shakes and Woodstock windows. They are a healthy lot, as islanders tend to be, for those who need more complicated medical services than mission hospitals provide drift away.

Opposite: Pleasure boats lie reflected in the calm waters of Ganges Harbour early in the morning on Saltspring Island, British Columbia.

There had been a drought the year I was there, and I brought the rain that ended it with me. I sat with a crowd in Betty's Café to get out of the weather and discovered that they were celebrating the fact that it was now safe to run an electric saw in the forest: the fire warnings were gone, and the real business, the business of logging off some of the best timber left in Canada, could begin again. I discovered that the people I was talking to were not hippies but city boys who had turned themselves into big businessmen, dealing in contracts in hundreds of thousands for thinning isolated stands of timber.

The one advertised tourist attraction of the islands is the golden spruce, an albino tree near the Yakoun River, a fine salmon stream. It stands in the bush near Port Clements, between Queen Charlotte City and Masset. Port Clements was, when I saw it, a collection of sodden houses sinking into a mush of dried fir needles and wet clay. Between Port Clements and Queen Charlotte City, the road runs along the east coast, past the strangely evocative Indian graveyard at Skidegate, by trees viciously bent westwards and a stony coast. Here, however, there are some sweeping stretches of farmland, and there has been for some time a successful cattle ranch at Tlell.

Masset is one of the most curious towns I have ever seen. It is situated on a long inlet and contains both a marina and a serious fishing harbour. Its buildings are on the whole functional and without charm, except for a new housing development that announces the presence of a Canadian Armed Forces base. The cannery looks as if it is falling into the sea; there are a couple of truncated totem poles outside the RCMP office, which look as if the Mounties had made them themselves from a kit; and there's a wind sock outside a white bungalow that announces the presence of the local airline office. In the rain, it's not a pretty town, and it usually rains here.

Farther on up the inlet, towards the open sea and North Beach, is the village of Haida. I squelched up there in the rain to see if there was anything left of the Old Masset I knew from Emily Carr's paintings. There are a couple of kilometres of numbered once-white bungalows in various states of disrepair and a small monument to Charles Edenshaw, the great chief and carver. Finally, I found a building marked "Museum" and stood, dripping with rain and weariness, in front of a glass case full of great stone phalluses. The room vibrates with a primitivism that must have shocked the missionaries.

It is the charm of the Charlottes to realize that although they are very new to our civilization, they once housed an old and noble culture. As you bob by little islands in boats, you know that some of them have been, as Maude Island was, Indian cemeteries. As you walk through Old Masset, now rechristened Haida, you remember photographs from the turn of the century showing every house with a landing stage and a totem pole. These have now decayed, fallen down, been carted off to museums. Haida culture was oral, evanescent, a cultural sack made of rhubarb leaves; and it is only now, when it is too late, that attempts are being made to understand and value it. At Skidegate and Masset there are still basket weavers and silver and argillite carvers (argillite having replaced the scrimshaw work visiting sailors taught the Haida to do), but there are no more of the beautiful sea-otter capes which visiting explorers purchased so cheaply and easily from the Haida. The few items in the museum at Old Masset are a pale reflection of the huge collections in Vancouver, Victoria, London, Paris. But there are mysterious and powerful reverberations on these islands: the death of a culture leaves behind it the same romantic plangency as the death of a beloved king.

It is easier to place and romanticize the Haida than any other Canadian Indian tribe. Their oral history has been recorded by ethnographers and turned into children's books by industrious West Coast writers. Their iconography has been appropriated by the British Columbia government to enhance the tourist trade. Their kinship systems, studied and admired in Europe, have been changed by Anglo-Saxon laws, and the Hudson's Bay blanket early replaced the sea-otter cloaks. Forced by promulgators of modern sanitation systems to abandon the habit of burying their dead in trees, they invented the custom of burying them in kerfed and ochred cedar boxes; these, too, are now being carried to museums. Loggers pick over what they can find of ancient sites; anthropologists and archaeologists quarrel over who has the right to dig where for Haida artifacts. It is amazing that the people themselves survive; and not surprising to hear that they find whites funny.

I had the great good luck, in my rainy peregrinations in Old Masset, to meet Robert Davidson, foremost among the current generation of carvers. It was he who made the new totem pole in front of Old Masset church, and he took me to Shark House, where with his brother and two apprentices he was making poles for the new longhouse which has since been erected by Heritage Canada.

There were four great poles prone on sawhorses and a strong sweet smell of red cedar shavings. Robert ran his hands over a pole and found a bad gouge on the thigh of a frog-figure.

"How're you going to fix it?" I asked.
"Crazy glue," he grinned.
"Does it weather?"
"We'll find out."

He took me to his house, which seemed like all the other shabby frame houses on the reserve until I stepped into a white-painted studio-cum-living-room that was as sophisticated as any in Toronto or New York. Half a dozen of us sat down and ate spaghetti. The Haida were tall, smooth, vital people, with straight features and the same merry eyes Emily Carr used to talk about. They'd all been silk-screening T-shirts. They had supplied enough for the Ravens but were behind on the Eagles. A dealer who was there explained that all Haida are either Ravens or Eagles and that they are excellent customers for their own people's work. He had been farther south buying jewellery from the Kwakiutl carvers — Eagles and Ravens again.

Davidson talks to me about the Indian craft industry in British Columbia, as he does so caressing with his restless hands a carving of a canoe that is smooth as glass. The bracelets they carve were originally made from tooled and flattened silver dollars. The old women are still making baskets and some people are doing well in halibut fishing, but, on the whole, things up here are still depressed. It's been a long time since Haida/Masset was a town of kings and slaves, war canoes and enormous potlatches. Not long ago, Davidson says, the Canadian forces' detachment marched through Masset with fixed bayonets and its colonel was presented by the mayor with the key to the town. And the base is on Indian land. I look at him and I think, art can save a few, but sometimes they must wonder who they are carving for and whether they should.

Time and space have their own eternities in the Charlottes. I walk through the English cemetery, its huge trees overgrown with a fungus of moss, to North Beach, a great grey empty stretch facing Alaska. I try to wade, but the water is glacial. I think of the pamphlets I have read that advertise the good life in the islands in terms of a place where food — and magic mushroom — gathering is still possible. The climate is relatively mild for the latitude indeed, but I know that endless exploiters and explorers have come here to mine and to farm and to fish, and gone empty-handed away.

I think of the man that Davidson told me about who had found the skeleton of a whale and spent weeks burying it in the forest.

"Why?" I asked.

"Oh, you can get a lot for a good skeleton from a museum. But it has to be intact. You don't want some idiot beachcombing half the vertebrae."

The Charlottes are for a very special kind of survivor, one who loves their bays and outcrops and secret places enough to take apart and put together a whole whale in order to stay on them.

At the turn of the century the B.C. government advertised land for sale here, open and unsurveyed. The newcomers nearly perished; the old hands had to pitch in to keep them alive. These are tough islands, isolated, rocky and wet. To live on them, you have to be fit, impervious to discomfort and moodiness and rain, subject in the right way to emanations of place.

I left Masset in a little plane with pink plush settees for seats; it slid down the sandbar, skimmed partway under the water, and then splashed up into the air. Suddenly the islands were distant triangles lying behind us in the water like teeth. I left wondering how the remaining Indians could stand us who brought them smallpox in return for otter cloaks, and exile to mission schools in return for their land.

The fact is, we like our artists and our Indians better dead; that way we get out of having to take the bitter with the sweet.

The Inside Passage

This natural, protected waterway extends up the coast of British Columbia and southeastern Alaska. The Canadian portion of the passage is generally taken to begin just south of Bella Bella.

For those who are not yachtsmen or pilots of small aircraft, many of the islands of the British Columbia coast remain inaccessible. There is, however, a route to Prince Rupert and the Alaska coast serviced by touring ships. *The Queen of Prince Rupert* is one of the Canadian ones, and it leaves from the same dock at Tsawwassen, south of Vancouver airport, as the ferries which go to the Gulf Islands.

The passage itself is sheltered from the open Pacific by a series of large islands that are really cut-off mountains of the Coast Range, and the visiting ships transport goods and services to places like Bella Bella, Bella Coola, and Ocean Falls, as well as showing tourists the real grandeur of the coast.

The farther north you go, the emptier the islands and the grander the scenery. Great white mountains loom down, whales and porpoises follow the ship; the shores of the islands are cluttered with so many deadheads one finally understands that the only thing to do is stand some of them up and make totem poles. If you want to see mountains, this is the way to do it; it's as exciting as flying across the Rockies and Selkirks on a clear blue day: you are far enough away to get a view.

Tiny airplanes loop in and out between the fiords and the scattered, mostly Indian, settlements. Some of the islands are very large — Princess Royal is one of the biggest — but few show any signs of habitation. There are totem poles to see at Alert Bay and a few abandoned canneries along the route. You'd have to be a barnacle to attach yourself here.

The Gulf Islands

The Gulf Islands consist of a scattering of a dozen large and a hundred or so small islands in the Strait of Georgia on the ferry route between Vancouver and Victoria. The largest is Saltspring, which has a considerable farming community; other islands are Mayne, North and South Pender, Saturna, Thetis, and Galiano. Farther north, also technically in the strait, are islands such as Hornby, Gabriola, Texada, and Valdes. While these are not officially Gulf Islands, they participate in the same history and share their beauty. Where they are sheltered by Vancouver Island from Pacific wind systems, they have the mildest winter climate in Canada.

Even in the blazing heat of a dry July, this path through the woods on Galiano is cool; shaded by giant fir trees, underneath which giant ferns spread prehensile arms, it skirts a little mountain and has not been logged for many years. In the clearings, giant raspberry bushes shelter the pressed-down grass beds that the mule deer make at night. Sometimes I hear them leaping into the underbrush as I pass. I walk carefully, for, true to its tropical-seeming nature, Galiano produces very large slugs, long brown-and-olive creatures who lie in the path, hoping for moisture in the indented tracks of the deer. In the woods, too, are fallen birch and enormous clutches of bamboo grass: one expects dinosaurs to emerge from the drying ooze. I know there are nuthatches and warblers in the trees, but I cannot see them. Like the deer, they are alert for trespassers in their kingdom. The only tame creature I ever met on this path was in fact an editor for the University of Toronto Press.

The Gulf Islands seem naturally to be the friends of artists, craftsmen, and intellectuals. Their climate is mild, their wild and beautiful shores are a stimulus to the imagination, and they are close enough to Vancouver and Victoria to provide access to books and art supplies and typewriter ribbons.

They are, alas, also very much in danger of overexploitation. Well served by the British Columbia Ferries, they have become attractive as real estate to frozen Albertans (if you see an Alberta driver, climb a tree, they say on Galiano) and brazen Vancouver speculators. They are the closest thing Canada has to Hawaii, and when the ferry debouches a thousand cars on a Friday night one shudders for their future.

Their past is a pretty one, though it is quickly sliding away. Although there are small Indian reserves on Galiano, Pender, and Mayne — and wonderful petroglyphs (one of a bear) on Saltspring Island — the Indian presence is not strong here as it is in the islands farther north. Rather, one looks around them and realizes that they have been populated by wave after wave of exiles and endowed with many dreams.

For the most part, they are formed of limestone, shale, and conglomerate, and offer many excellent harbours and curious rock formations. They were first explored by the Spaniards in the eighteenth century as they worked their way up from California, leaving their names on islands like Valdes and Gabriola, on Trincomali Channel and Virago Point. Then, when the English came, they were seized upon as ideal places to farm and raise children. The climate seemed almost as balmy as Cornwall's, the land capable of being cleared of its salal bushes and leaning arbutus (madroña) trees for cosy little farms. Saltspring, the largest of the islands, was quickly laid out in farms, and the few native islanders one meets speak happily of childhoods spent insouciantly rowing from island to island for picnics and barn raisings and house warmings.

Many of these settlers were not, however, born farmers. They tended to be ladies and gentlemen, and they found the life hard, especially when it seemed necessary to send the children to the mainland to boarding school or hire nannies to educate them. Sheep farming was the most profitable — especially during the days of the famous smuggler who sold the shearings for a better price over the line in the San Juan Islands.

These people were remittance men on the whole: although they were often as respectable as a brass doorknocker, they were subsidized by money from home. Galiano, Saltspring, and North Pender were scattered with gentry and younger sons. Lord Loughborough was sent to Thetis Island to learn farming when he was twenty. Galiano was seen as a British squirearchy by the rougher settlers who had come earlier. On Saltspring Island, Henry Wright Bullock in 1892 built himself a large house and acquired fourteen orphanage boys as servants. He treated them well, gave grand parties, and instructed the local girls in the art of dress and deportment.

Not many of the English settlers' fortunes lasted as long as Squire Bullock's. Captain Eustace Maude might not have foreseen when he left England that he would eventually run the Point Comfort Hotel on Mayne Island, a popular resort until about 1925 when it was bought by an eccentric Englishwoman and renamed Culzean Castle. Yet living in style was cheap for a long time, for at the turn of the century Mr. Gerald Mayne built himself a very large colonial bungalow of the sort you find in Australia and the Mediterranean (and in eastern Canada too) for the sum of $1,800. The mild, rainy climate, island shores studded with mussels and oysters and gorgeous orange and purple starfish, ravens of a size that seem no longer to exist outside Shakespeare, basking sea lions, must have seemed paradise.

Alas, paradise was not quite enough for the English settlers. They were neither trained farmers nor peasant enough to live off the little that they could grow. Their children admit to having been more interested in boating than in getting an education. They did not establish a new landed gentry in the gulf.

They did, however, establish a number of good traditions, for on Saltspring you can buy some of the finest spring lamb in the world. There are apple orchards and boat builders, and there survives in the Gulf Islands a love of nature and of animals (though not always garden-munching deer) which is peculiar to the English and endearing now they are our masters no more.

Two other immigrant colonies came and left little evidence of their passing. Blacks settled on Saltspring when it was one of the termini of the Underground Railroad. The Japanese came, fished energetically, set up wonderful market gardens, and became valued members of the communities on Mayne and Saltspring. The internment camps ended that. Every history has its bitterness, but this is a particularly sharp one, for no group grooms a garden or a fishery more carefully than the Japanese.

The islands underwent another invasion in the sixties, this time by the so-called hippies. Sadly, for those of us who hoped they might invent a new way to live, some left ruin behind them: their dream of the simple life was not based on information, they coped badly with fire and sanitation, and a little begging led to a lot of unauthorized long-distance calls. Now, frames for abandoned geodesic domes and ruins of burnt shacks are all that are left of the improvised communes, though a number of bright young artists, who do know how to manage this fragile world, followed in their footsteps and enlivened Gulf Islands society.

These islands are a haven for individualists as well as for Calgary capitalists and the descendants of the English settlers. Some of the most self-determined people I know live here. They are people who have worked out their value systems and their relations to communities very carefully, balancing individuality against involvement as they raise herbs, paint pictures, write books and plays and music. For them, raven-croaking winter is the magic time, when the roads are free mostly of tourists and snow, and when quiet settles in like fog. A good many of them are women whose names are very well known. You meet them not at fancy parties but when the volunteer fire brigade is called out.

The major islands are served by the B.C. Ferries service. The smaller ones tend towards private ownership. An American bought Wallace and wrote two books about it; Elvis Presley is said to have owned one, and another was given to Princess Margaret on a royal visit. It is now a nature preserve. D'Arcy Island, close to Sidney, was a leper colony until 1924 when the lepers were moved to Bentinck, nearer Victoria. That operation was closed in 1956. A friend of mine described sitting in a foetal position in a leper's cell, staring out at deserted graves and feeling cold all over. One wonders if there are lepers now and where they go.

As the ferry steams towards them, the islands, flat on the horizon, straighten their shoulders and rise out of the water. Gulls wheel, cormorants leave their post perches, eagles sail away. Passengers lean over the rail and fix their eyes on the ascending ramps by the timber-cluttered beaches. The dividing line between islanders and tourists is the skin and the luggage: the nut-brown ones are carrying window panes, art supplies, boxes of beer.

The ferry shudders and halts. Queen Elizabeth, faded in her frame, smiles down at an emptying lounge. Dogs are called to heel. Islanders on the ramp spread their arms like sails to catch swarms of visiting children. Cars rumble out of the belly of the ship, headed for the sand beaches of Hornby, the far stretches of Saturna, the round pock-marked inlets, where under the complaints of mewing eaglets the children can throw kelp at each other, push deadheads against tide and wave, pretend they own the whole world. The people who winter on the islands cross their fingers, hoping the city folk won't drain the water table dry.

The Islands of the Great Lakes

Once, just once, flying from Edmonton to Toronto in the spring, I saw what could unexaggeratedly be called the sight of my life.

As usual, the sky was cloudy over Manitoba and the Lake of the Woods, and I started reading again, despairing; then, just as we came over Lake Superior, the weather cleared and we were, just, well, there, flying into the sunset. Isle Royale lay exactly like its skeletal outline on the map, naked below me, and I hurried to the opposite window and I think I even saw St. Ignace Island. And we were rushing to the great bowknot that ties the lakes together, the Sault: so I saw Lake Superior rushing into Whitefish Bay and Batchawana, and then the St. Marys River and the twin cities; and St. Joe, dear St. Joe; Sugar, Drummond, Cockburn, Manitoulin; and darned if, still in the flowing coloured light, we didn't, attempting to find Toronto, follow down the Bruce with every island backlit like something out of a travel movie, so I saw Cove Island light, the Flowerpot Islands, and even the whitecaps on Nottawasaga Bay.

Down, zooming home, over the Rocky Saugeen River and Holstein Pond, which wouldn't be big enough to be called a slough in Alberta; then, in the dark, to the big vulgar necklace of light over Toronto. There never was such a coming home.

When the map in your mind and the earth meet, bliss exists.

St. Joseph Island

Situated just to the southeast of Sault Ste. Marie, St. Joseph Island noses into the St. Marys River at its northern end and extends well into Lake Huron on its southeastern shores. It is joined to the mainland by a causeway. On the island's southern tip are the remains of a fort which used to be an important base of operations in the Upper Great Lakes. It was destroyed by the Americans during the War of 1812 but is now being restored.

St. Joseph Island holds a wealth of history — it was a meeting place of the Indian nations and a headquarters of the Indian Department — but it is most notorious for the story of an early British settler, Major William Kingdom Rains, who formed a company to purchase it in 1834. He invested in five thousand acres of land at a shilling an acre on condition that he bring settlers in, then built a steamship called the *Simcoe*, and arrived in 1835.

Rains was no businessman; he had served in the British forces during the Napoleonic Wars, been stationed in Sicily where he met Byron, married, and returned much-decorated to his native Wales after peace was declared. Casting about for work (and the competition for a place amongst halfpay officers must have been fierce) he got a job as one of the investigators in the preface to the trial of Queen Caroline, George IV's scandalous wife, and developed a conjugal dislike of his own. His life was further complicated by the fact that his friend Mad Jack Doubleday — a lawyer in Milford Haven who was imprisoned for debt — entrusted his two beautiful daughters, Frances and Eliza, to him. Rather than see them go into service in a public house, which was their alternative, Rains took them both to be his mistresses, and having failed to prove useful in the drawing-office of his cousin, the great engineer Isambard Kingdom Brunel, he hired a ship and took the whole lot of his dependants (by this time Fanny had two babies) to Canada.

He left, it appears, his legal wife in York and took land at Sutton, on Lake Simcoe, to which he was entitled as a British officer. Local opinion has it that it was his desire to escape the censure of an increasing population that sent him in 1835 to Lake Huron; but he had always wanted to own an island.

The trading company failed, but the family increased magnificently. I have seen the ruins of two of Rains's establishments on St. Joseph Island; it's obvious that as the children increased, so did the need for space, and it was easy to move to a new bay. Eventually, there were nineteen children, all of whom grew up to be great workers, for, as legend has it, the major was more of an administrator than a worker. After a certain point, they built separate wings on the cabins for the two families, and as civilization and moral censure moved nearer, they settled Eliza's family in a cabin which still stands on Sugar Island, now part of Michigan.

I once tried to collect material for a life of the major, but alas he stopped keeping even a notebook when he arrived on St. Joseph Island. However, it became obvious from his peregrinations that he was frantically trying to find a location that would provide sustenance for his offspring. The summer climate was good, and the island's nearness to Sault Ste. Marie meant that provisions could be brought in, but as for a living — the trading post failed, there wasn't enough water at Milford Haven for a mill, and life seems to have been a scramble. Fanny and Eliza made all the children's clothes of course, and Rains educated the children himself from textbooks which the families still own, but he did not become a grand gentleman there, let alone a feudal lord.

His children, however, spread up and down the lakes as pilots, lumber dealers, navigators, and lighthouse keepers. His oldest son, Owen, was known as the finest cornerman on the island when it came to putting up cabins, and wonderful stories are told of Rainses who stayed there and on Sugar, and became the great characters of the neighbourhood.

Towards the end of his life, the English major's livelihood was made by supplying cordwood to steamers plying the narrow channel between his home at Sailor's Encampment and Neebish Island. They say the ships' bands used to strike up "God Save the Queen" when they passed his dock. He probably also, at various points, kept a tavern. When he died, his body was taken by sailboat to Sault Ste. Marie for a grand funeral.

Rains's children left a considerable posterity behind, and I went up there one summer to collect stories from them. I heard sentences like, "They lived all winter on turnips and fish, and were full of pep and ginger in the spring." "They all lived to be old. Owen was ninety-six. He used to read Dickens to Victoria, his wife, who couldn't read and write. That's why Tudor was always called Pip."

They yarned on. There was a time, they said, when they didn't like to talk about the major and his scandalous life; the half sisters and brothers had always said they were cousins. But, looking back now, the way things have changed, they realized that Fanny and Eliza would have perished without each other and it didn't matter so much any more, did it? Eliza's son Big Allan became lighthouse keeper on Sugar Island and was always known as Allan the Giant. There was a daughter called Sara Snowdrop. Fanny's daughter Linda married the man who drew up the border, which put half the family in a different country.

One of them, while showing me an album containing a recipe for raspberry shrub, written in exquisite Regency handwriting, asked me what I'd heard the major had died of. When I said "diabetes" three others nodded sadly. Blanche, who was ninety-one and had taught school in Baltimore, said to Earl, who was ninety and lived in Nebraska, "Earl, I'll lay you out." They were grandchildren.

"You've come too late," Blanche said to me. "I've forgotten it all now." But she remembered good things — summer boating, ice-cream parties at the Encampment when they had the hotel. And also the terrible danger in spring when the men set out to walk across the ice to get to their jobs on the boats in Detour and Petoskey in Michigan. "Linda lost her husband that way. We call it gob-ice and slob-ice when it's like that. I guess he went right through."

The median age of the citizens of St. Joseph Island is very high now. In the summer, it's beautiful northern country. One woman told me she thought it was the major who brought the hops and the raspberries that grow wild everywhere. Someone chimed in that it was the major who planted the Lombardy poplars that grow there.

Mostly, now, the island exists for farming and tourism. Its beaches are fine and the water is still and clear. There's the fort to visit and there are said to be ruins at Milford Haven, though all I could ever find was a chimney that looked far too new. A few people I met live there all year round and commute to jobs in the Soo, and there are still good farms and market gardens, one with a round barn, and a sugar industry. The big lakers steam by and practically lift St. Joseph Island off its moorings. I wonder what the sailors would think if they saw the ghost of the last of the Regency bucks lifting his now-shabby hat to them.

Manitoulin and the Islands of Georgian Bay

Manitoulin Island, in Lake Huron northwest of Georgian Bay, is the largest freshwater island in the world, a triangular formation some 150 kilometres long and 60 kilometres in breadth at its widest point. To the west of Manitoulin lies Cockburn Island and to the southeast lies Fitzwilliam, while in Georgian Bay itself there is a large variety of islands of all shapes and forms: the curious limestone formations known as the Flowerpot Islands; the Thirty Thousand Islands stretching down the bay's eastern shore; isolated outcrops like Lonely Island; and, in the south, Christian, Beckwith, Giants Tomb, Beausoleil, and the others of Georgian Bay Islands National Park.

Many of us who grew up in Ontario have discrete perceptions of these islands, and there seems to be no way to reconcile them. They contain some of the great cottage country in the world, famous for pike and bass and sturgeon fishing; they also resonate with the violent vision of the Group of Seven painters, who caught the magnificence and unruliness of both lake and landscape in their twisted visions of islands and lakes and jackpine. The islands are thus an extension of the resort area in the Muskoka Lakes and Algonquin Park. But if you approach them either from the Sudbury area or from the Penetang peninsula, you realize that they are as rich in Indian and French history as any part of the country, and the result is sometimes confusing.

The Martyrs' Shrine and the reconstructed forts near Midland remind us of the torture and martyrdom of the good Jesuits Brébeuf and Lalemant by the Iroquois in 1649. Having been brought up a rabid Protestant, I for years thought it was called ''Martha's shrine'' and dismissed the place from my mind, though I enjoyed singing Brébeuf's Christmas carol. Where Jesuit history intersects with island history is after the martyrdom, when the remaining Huron Indians, chased by their enemies to Christian Island from the rolling agricultural country of Simcoe County, retreated in a hopeless attempt to survive as a people. Christian Island was not large enough to feed their five thousand. They debated moving to Manitoulin, but the growing season was shorter there by just long enough to prevent them from raising their traditional crops of corn and squash and beans: some stayed on Christian Island, protected by the Jesuit fort whose ruins can still be discerned there (and which in turn is protected by massasauga rattlers, for in every paradise there is a snake!); others took the long trek through the French River system to Québec City, where they were settled on the Île d'Orléans.

The islands of Georgian Bay lie at the junction of the continent's major trade routes; in earlier centuries Indians came from the north with copper down the myriad river systems that connect Algoma with the lakes; from the east through the Ottawa system, and up the Great Lakes via the Ohio and Mississippi River systems. This was rich fur-trading country, central to the mid-continent Native people's culture. Here the Hurons, a stable agricultural people, traded their agricultural produce for wampum from the oceans, and furs and copper from farther north and west.

Champlain and his successors from other European countries were only too delighted to discover the great inland seas and their rich existing commerce. For centuries, large Manitoulin and its American neighbour, little Michilimackinac, were the centre of a flourishing trade in fur and weapons.

The Indian presence is still strong in the area and probably best accounted for by remembering that Hemingway's Indian stories took place on a mainland not very far from here and that Longfellow wrote *Hiawatha* on one of the little islands between Cockburn and St. Joseph. Indeed, one of the chiefs of the Sucker Creek reserve obtained work in New York playing Hiawatha on stage in the 1880s.

By that time, the old way was gone and northern Ontario was being opened up to mining and smelting and agriculture. The fur-bearing animals moved farther north and west, and what Indians were left were herded onto reserves, including the very large unceded Wikwemikong on Manitoulin, where one's liberal lawyer friends often find work now.

I went to summer camp on Beausoleil, a beautiful hook-shaped island off Honey Harbour, spent a good deal of time lying on hot rocks (never mind sand beaches: it's hot Georgian Bay rocks that melt the core of the winter from the body), and paddling down channels full of pickerelweed and water lilies. Like the thousands of cottagers and holiday-makers around us, we were careful of open water: Champlain's *Mer Douce* has moments of great violence, as numerous accounts of lake shipwrecks attest; anyway, *douce* refers to the fact that the water is not saline.

But it is Manitoulin rather than the islands farther south that seems most to attest to the Indian continuity. I have a theory that we become more accepting of the Native people the more generations we are from Europe; my generation could not weigh in like the Jesuits and simply attempt to lift a people from its culture, because we have read about and half-absorbed that culture, and believe it really is one; but I have met new immigrants in Toronto who still speak of Indians as "savages" and fail to see why special arrangements are made for them. Perhaps they have no guilt — their ancestors, after all, were not the ones who took their land or enforced the rules which that taking involved.

But I would like to send those critics up to Manitoulin on a May or June evening; not to the reserves, where a certain amount of bear-walking still goes on, as well as politicking; not to the central high school, where the principal speaks of "our ancestors the pioneers" to those whose ancestors were anything but; not to Providence Bay, home of my grandfather's great friend, Dr. Mutchmor, for half a century leader of the Temperance Union; but to the sad, silver shores of the inland lakes of Manitoulin.

Here, in the spring, it seems to me that always just one bird is singing. Fish leap at incessant mosquitoes, the flowers are beginning to come out, the sun is setting. And you are reminded just by the stillness, the flat quietness, that Manitoulin is in legend the home of Gitchi Manitou, the greatest of the Indian gods. And of Matchi Manitou, who is evil.

It is easy to be tolerant at a distance, where the different ways of the Native people are not interfering with one's own basically nineteenth-century, busy-making ways. But it's possible, isn't it, that the bay and the islands are permeated by a spirituality which, however far it is from the Indo-European one, still pervades both the high escarpment and the flatlands in its shadow.

Listen: you can hear the birds talking it all out on Manitoulin on a spring evening.

The Fishing Islands

This archipelago of some fifteen islets lies in Lake Huron to the west of the Bruce Peninsula, between Oliphant and Red Bay.

These islands are commercially insignificant I am sure and now hold only a few summer cottages, but when I was a child, spending summers on the shore across from them, they seemed a great source of mystery. My father and a friend once rescued two fishermen who had been ship-wrecked on them — better to bring home a story than a string of bass, I thought. Sunset Island, the smallest, was so near the shore you could swim to it, and the first time I did I thought I'd be in the Olympics.

Main Station Island, the largest and farthest south, contains the ruins of what was once thought to be a fort; but it has proved to be the remains of Captain Alex MacGregor's fishing station, from which in the palmy days of the Great Lakes fishery three thousand barrels of whitefish and herring were sent to Detroit. MacGregor, an American, was ousted by a bunch of patriots from Goderich who included the famous Dr. William "Tiger" Dunlop. Their operation failed in 1848.

I was taken out there once when I was shorter than the poison ivy that grew along the deserted paths; there were the ruins of a few cabins, fringed gentians grew there, and it seemed old and spooky. Indian legend has it that the Fishing Islands are haunted, which probably means that some of the group were used as cemeteries by the Chippewa and Neutrals in the region.

Years later I saw an advertisement in a Toronto paper for the sale of Wild Man Island, and, answering it for the purpose of research rather than purchase, discovered that the American owner was a descendant of the Durand family who settled in southwestern Ontario in the seventeenth century. That name of course has worked its way throughout southwestern Ontario, from the Bruce to Sarnia and Windsor, and indicates a French history of the province that went unacknowledged in my day — just in case they were Catholics.

It's occasionally still possible to buy salt herring and fresh lake trout and whitefish at Southampton, but the grand days of the Great Lakes fishery are now over, for where lamprey control has succeeded, acid rain and pollution have taken over.

Pelee Island

Apart from its neighbour, tiny Middle Island, Pelee is the most southern place in Canada. It lies at the west end of Lake Erie, about halfway between the Canadian and American shores, and it is by far the largest island in the lake— approximately 14 by 6 kilometres in size.

At first, it exists only as an eyebrow of fuzz on the horizon; you are preoccupied with the fact that Lake Erie is shallow and as rough as the Gulf of St. Lawrence. As you approach, it does not rise up to greet you, for Pelee is a flat island, saucer-shaped really, a plain little plateau only slightly elevated from the lake bed. In the autumn, when it receives most of its visitors, it is golden with its southwestern Ontario preponderance of oak, ash, hackberry and hickory.

The docks are businesslike. Tourism is important, but not nearly so important as the soybean industry, which was pioneered here in the thirties. The enthusiastic town clerk will tell you that at that time Pelee produced seventy-five per cent of Ontario's soy. Right now the shoulders of the roads are lined with trucks waiting to fill the laker *New York News* with the spherical beans.

Within the next fortnight, twenty thousand ring-necked pheasants will be released during the two-week-long session of the annual pheasant hunt, and the island will be turned into a vast and somewhat dangerous hotel, every permanent resident putting up and feeding as many of the sixteen hundred visitors as he can, the Pelee Club and the few motels filled to the bursting point.

No sound but gunfire; and then. . .silence. The restaurants will close, the caretakers of the club will go to Florida, the island treasury will be fifty or sixty thousand dollars richer. When freeze-up comes, even the ferries will go away. The 283 citizens, except those who are in high school and boarding in Kingsville, will return to quiet lives, isolated, private, on their own again.

They are used to this life. Many of them are descendants of the romantic William McCormick who settled his family on Pelee in 1834, having acquired the lease ten years earlier from Thomas McKee's son, who got it from his father, who got it from "the sachems and chiefs of the Chippewa and Ottawa Nations" to whom he was to pay three bushels of Indian corn every year.

Little is known of McKee, but McCormick's grandfather fought in the Battle of the Boyne and was Scots-Irish. His son Alexander ventured to America and became a fur trader in Ohio, near the present site of Toledo. There he became enamoured of a Miss Elizabeth Turner, who had been captured by the Wyandot Indians. Having failed to ransom her, he smuggled her away in the bottom of a canoe under a load of furs. They had a family and continued to operate their trading post until, as United Empire Loyalists, they settled on the Canadian side of the St. Clair River near Colchester.

William was their oldest son and has, according to a Pelee history written by a descendant, a good many firsts to his credit: he was the first postmaster in Colchester and the first man married by a clergyman in Canada West. The fact that he and his wife had thirteen children seems to me to have some bearing on his need to purchase a whole island for his family.

In some ways, theirs was the usual pioneer idyll — the business of transporting livestock, building docks, raising children in the wilds, quarrying stone and cutting wood (some of the stone went into the Welland Canal, and the wood was used for building and stoking ships), preserving in summer what would keep them in winter, sailing over to the mainland for what could not be made at home. Meanwhile, lots were sold off for cash, a stone house was put up, and a lighthouse and a church: the island was becoming a community as well as a family fief.

Pelee was, however, subject to interruptions of its bucolic existence. On February 26, 1838, three hundred American supporters of William Lyon Mackenzie captured the island. The McCormicks fled over the ice to Fort Malden and notified the British forces, who satisfactorily defeated the ingrates. Pelee suffered from the same problems most islands did then — lack of communication services, transport uncertainties, tragedies at sea. But it has traditionally been the home of agricultural experiment, and gradually mixed farming began to give over to the cultivation of those crops to which its southerly climate lent a certain glamour: tobacco, for instance, and grapes, which were first planted in 1866. Pelee's special problem was that it was low-lying and subject to flooding; an American, a Dr. Scudder after whom the port on the north side of the island is named, having travelled in the Netherlands, devised a system of drainage which eventually increased farming acreage considerably and is still in operation.

A large winery operated on the island in the nineteenth century; its products and proprietors were housed in a great mansion called Vin Villa, over the ruins of which wild grapes now climb. Recently an Austrian company has purchased 300 hectares of land to reclaim the industry.

There are a few cottages, mostly belonging to Americans. High lake levels in recent years have brought them dangerously close to falling in, and the periphery of the island is now barricaded with huge blocks of stone. The government has purchased parts of the island as nature reserves, for Pelee's varieties of birds and vegetation are as special as its southern location. The Pelee Club, a large white private establishment which names Abraham Lincoln's son as one of its founders, still houses rich sport fishermen and dines them at long tables under the glaring eye of Napoleon on flower-printed dishes reminiscent of all the old summer cottages in the world. They play English or American billiards on good slate tables, stack their rods in racks made for them when the club was set up in 1883. Grover Cleveland slept here, Marshall Field, judges and presidents and capitalists of all kinds. The private bowling alley has been turned into a locker room for their boat-motors, but one wonders now whether they dare eat their fish.

Pelee is a model island. It lies dreaming practical dreams under the eye of three nuclear power plants; once a week bankers arrive by helicopter from Kingsville to take in the cash, and although its population is a third of what it was in 1930 and there are few cultural activities, the people who remain there seem perfectly happy with their lot. The farming is good and so is the price for soy; in winter, they amuse themselves by snowmobiling to the American islands nearby; there is no doctor, but the sick are easily airlifted to Leamington and Kingsville, and the electricity cable from the mainland works most of the time.

The future is cloudy for some; there's regret that the high school has been closed and students have to leave to go beyond eighth grade: when they come back there isn't much to do. The island sits out in Lake Erie, small, southerly, self-contained and half-forgotten: exactly what most of its residents want it to be.

The Toronto Islands

This small archipelago in Toronto Harbour was originally the sandspit formed by the entry of the Don River into Lake Ontario, but in 1858 a storm cut a channel through the connecting arm of land. The major islands are Centre, Wards, Muggs, and Algonquin.

Although one is frequently warned not to live in the past, there are times when it is probably better to do so. On a hot August night in Toronto, you make your way down to a waterfront (much improved, it must be admitted, by large hotels and skyscraper condominiums and newspaper offices) to a modernized ferry dock, only to be forced into one of those revolving grills that cause you to KNOW that authority in Canada thinks you're a criminal; if you can bear to go through, you feel, then, the first breeze off the lake, and when the gates are pulled back you make your way not to the Gulag but to the pleasant deck of the *Thomas J. Rennie* or one of the other ferry boats which are to my mind the best in Canada.

And you go, haunted by pictures of your father in a straw boater playing a banjo and your mother leaning over in a cloche hat and a dress with a hip-sash, and the nearer you get to the shore, the sadder it is: things are not what they once were.

The Toronto Islands have been a major delight of the city since the area was settled; Mrs. Simcoe, wife of the first governor of Upper Canada, drew delightful sketches of Gibraltar Point. Since then, the islands have been deluged with visitors in summer and fought over by planners all winter.

They house, and have always housed, a number of yacht clubs, the Royal Canadian being the important one. Their inner lagoons form one long marina, and it's always worth walking them to see if the Chinese junk is still there. At the turn of the century there was a kind of tent city on Wards Island, as well as a big hotel. Gradually, this turned into a permanent settlement. At Hanlans Point, on the other end, there is a fun fair. And before the harbour was polluted, everybody used the beaches.

Now Wards Island is enveloped both in masonry (to protect it from erosion) and controversy, as the Parks Department of the city seeks to expel the permanent residents and turn the whole island into recreational lands. There's an odd left-wing right-wing split here, for in theory the left should be in favour of "the people" using the whole frontage the whole time. But Wards is a special sort of place, a real community, an alternate haven for those who want to live in the city yet apart from it; and permanent residents add a humanity to the islands which the Parks Department, for all its tailored gardening, can't quite manage.

The other permanent residents are a large flock of Canada geese, who find plenty of fodder in addition to the summer's popcorn and hamburger buns, and have decided to increase, multiply, and forget the way south. The signs say "Please Walk on the Grass" but you can't sit on it any more.

I go there once a year hoping, this time, not to turn into Scrooge, but I always do. The fun fair is clean and well organized and too expensive, the new architecture is so far from our ancestors' summer dreams that I prefer the gritty poverty of Cherry Beach across the water. But occasionally even these overvisited islands provide a touch of mystery — an enormous carp shadowed by the breakwater along the boardwalk, the cries of the coxswain as a rowing team passes on one of the inner channels.

Oh, I suppose the only thing to do with them is realize that the innocence has been gone for a hundred years and let the Parks Department have its way. Still, the islands are a document in the history of our ambivalence to change: protected by breakwaters and dredging, their shape is preserved; but we resist with shrill cries their being dragged into a modern world that makes too obvious the loveliness of the world we have lost.

The Thousand Islands

These are the islands that fill the St. Lawrence River between Cornwall and Kingston.

They are small, and few of them — except for Wolfe, Amherst, and Simcoe near Kingston — have permanent summer populations. The rest are crowned by summer cottages, joined by little romantic bridges, and much photographed by tourists from boats that run out of Gananoque. Cruising amongst them is a pleasure on a misty summer evening, for certain cottagers have obviously been rivals in creating picturesque summer home effects. Here, the Canadian Shield runs down into Lake Ontario and fragments itself in the river.

Farther north and west, the Shield is pockmarked with lakes and islands and cottages; the best of the summer houses run to the pattern of one I was once lent for a week, which had its own dock, three different small places to swim, and a grand verandah surrounding a great, drafty, frame house. There was a stone fireplace in the living room and a wood stove in the huge kitchen. The cupboards held old willow pattern dinnerware, enough for a couple of dozen. There were two conventional bedrooms, but the porches and upstairs remained basically dormitories: a huge family must have congregated there once.

The whole week I was there it rained; fortunately, the living room cupboards were stocked with *New Yorker*s — all the summer issues from the 1930s — so that I was able to lie idle, listening to rain drip into pails, and read Alexander Woollcott.

You find this basic Ontario-cottage form throughout the Thousand Islands, the Kawarthas, Haliburton, and the Muskokas: a bare comfort which gives you the idea that the cottage-banished second-best was very good indeed.

Farming is the main occupation on the larger islands. This, of course, has been jeopardized on Cornwall Island, where emissions from the aluminum factory across the river in New York are being investigated as causes of cattle disease. The cheese factory on Amherst Island, a favourite summer destination of Kingstonians, burned down some time ago, but there are still pleasant farms and pleasanter beaches in the area. I met a helicopter pilot from Wolfe when I was on Pelee Island, who shook his head and said, yes, the young people were going away — for jobs, for city amenities. The soil on the Shield is thin here, and poor farming will not hold this generation on the land.

The international border goes through the Thousand Islands, which means that some of the biggest ones are American. On one of these is the enormous Boldt Castle, a millionaire's dream of a Loire Chateau. It's open for tourists now. I'm afraid it gives me the shudders: all those rooms to sweep, I think, and not even fifteenth century; but it's a sensational sight.

Montréal
and Surrounding Islands

Île de Montréal and Île Jésus are the two main islands on which the city now stands, though there are two other large islands nearby — Île Bizard and Île Perrot — and many smaller ones.

At times, Montréal is only another city, Frencher than most, but basically a big modern city with its park on the top and a great electric cross to remind us that this is not Orangeman's territory. You don't often perceive it as a group of islands when you're in it, not unless you're trying to get through a tunnel or across a bridge on a summer weekend, and then suddenly this isn't Los Angeles or Toronto or Sydney: it's an island city.

Then there are other times, flicking through the suburbs on the train when it rattles across bridges and the winking islands of the Lake of Two Mountains appear, or when you're driving in the country in the winter and you're suddenly aware that at the edge of the road there is ice; or, of course, farther downriver, when you're driving beside a laker: then you know you're on an island.

Of all the Canadian island groups, Montréal is the most important commercially and the most illustrative historically of the conflict between French and English ideas of how to live, a conflict which quickly won over Iroquois and Algonquin Indian ideas of what to do with their ancient camp of Hochelaga.

The city of Montréal itself, which now dominates the whole archipelago, is interesting in that it grew from the vision of the Abbé Olier in Paris, who sent Paul de Chomedey de Maisonneuve to New France to found a great mission to the "Red Men." Maisonneuve landed at Île de Montréal on May 18, 1642, and quickly realized the strategic situation of Olier's dream colony. A palisaded fortress sprang up, and seigniorial rights to a great deal of the island were granted to the Sulpicians, "the Gentlemen of the Seminary" whose two grey towers later marked the pleasantest stretch of Sherbrooke Street.

The city was soon as famous for its activities in the fur trade as it was for religious establishments and for the activities of Marie-Marguerite d'Youville, founder of the Grey Nuns order. Reading French and English histories of the island city is a schizophrenic experience, the emphasis of the former being entirely devoted to the great religious enterprises and the exploits of the Iberville brothers against the Iroquois, and that of the latter on the growing capitalism of the fur traders of both the Hudson's Bay and North-West companies. Needless to say, all establishments prospered in their way, and, until recently, Montréal was a city of great limestone mansions and great limestone convents and seminaries.

Nuns Island is suburban development now; the Sherbrooke Street mansions one by one have become office towers and apartment hotels. "Old" Montréal, at least that part that remains, has been restored in a peculiarly English way to the great benefit of the tourist trade, and to get any maritime sense of the place you have to belong to the Pointe Claire Yacht Club.

Occasionally, however, it is possible to discern the islands' past; there are still byways on Île Jésus, and still glimpses off St. James Street of Lombardy poplars that stand by the Sulpicians' original walls. The little sailors' church, Notre Dame de Bonsecours, blocked as it is from the water by great grain elevators, preserves relics of the pious times when a voyage to Montréal by sea was perilous and to be prayed over.

But it is mostly the little islands, however rearranged and destroyed they are, that preserve touches of the past. Île Dorval, for instance, just off the airport, was once the fief of the Abbé de Fénelon, who built a school there for Indian children. In 1854 Sir George Simpson of the Hudson's Bay Company acquired it and constructed an edifice grand enough to entertain Edward, Prince of Wales, during the opening of the Victoria Bridge in 1860.

The smiling islands southwest of Montréal are the beginning of the Thousand Islands system. Île Deslauriers and Saint-Ours, above the Lachine Rapids, were once considered to be fit to be set aside as nature reserves, but efforts have failed to save them from destruction by industry and by the enlargement of the canal systems that formed the St. Lawrence Seaway. Many of the small islands east of Montréal are in fact nothing more than garbage dumps, though there is some hope of rescuing a few of them for the proposed St. Lawrence Park. Île Sainte-Thérèse, where Charles Le Moyne was captured by the Iroquois, has been designated as an ecological park, and pleasant paths and picnic tables now exist among the remnants of earlier developments.

I always have a feeling that there is a vast and secret life among the reaches of the rivers that meet at Montréal. One senses both the anger and the magic of the people-within-a-people, the descendants of the habitants and seigneurs. Little islands and reedy reaches were certainly hideouts for draft-resisters during both the 1914 and the 1939 wars, when the French were appalled by conscription; one feels that however harsh the grip of the great nineteenth-century merchants of Montréal was, it was too coarse to encompass all the secret places of this delta-land and that perhaps, still, going north on the road to Oka, or sliding around the end of Île Jésus in a canoe, one might find a segment of La Salle's dream of China on the lost shore of a small neglected island.

Île d'Orléans

About 30 kilometres in length and 8 kilometres wide, Île d'Orléans lies in the St. Lawrence River just to the east of Québec City. It was discovered by Jacques Cartier when in 1535 he sailed up the river as far as Montréal.

Settled by immigrants from such French provinces as Poitou, Île d'Orléans is large and agreeable and not yet entirely a suburb of Québec City. In his enthusiasm, Cartier called it Île Bacchus for the wild grapes he found there. It was also temporarily named after Ste. Marie and St. Laurent, and briefly called Île des Sorciers. Like so many islands of eastern Canada, it changed hands several times before a permanent population was established in the late seventeenth century.

Île d'Orléans played a strong role in Québec religious history; it was visited by Bishop Laval and Mère Marie de l'Incarnation; its first church, which was built in 1669, was the third in Québec; and in 1685 Marguerite Bourgeoys established a convent here. The island was divided into eight pleasant seigneuries, and as the community settled down it produced farmers, sailors, river pilots, and fishermen. Its citizens also developed a reputation for having second sight — hence "Île des Sorciers."

In 1759, General Wolfe camped here before the Battle of the Plains of Abraham (the island's position is strategic for control of the St. Lawrence waterway). The British conquest did not affect the Orléanais profoundly, for by then they were well established in their agrarian and maritime ways. They continued to build beautiful stone houses and mills. Even in the 1920s they were considered to have maintained Québécois customs with great purity, still making their cloth and a good many of their other artifacts at home, continuing religious rituals long established (including a number of quarrels about relics of St. Paul and St. Clement), telling and retelling the old folk tales, preserving the legend of Madeleine de Verchères, whose mother came from Orléans, and heroic tales of attempts to deceive the British in battles of the 1750s.

Today, the island is joined to the mainland by a bridge. Its older character is preserved in the paintings of the Canadian Barbizon School, notably Horatio Walker. You can still find fine handicrafts here and, in July, the finest raspberries and strawberries in North America.

As you drive down the tree-lined roads, meditate on the fact that Île d'Orléans almost became the city of Montréal: the provincial governors wanted it that way, but Chomedey de Maisonneuve, who had dreamed in France of building a great city in the new territory, insisted on moving farther down the river to the island with the mountain on it.

Grosse Île/
Île de la Quarantaine

Although named "grosse," this is a small island,
less than 5 kilometres in length. It lies in the St.
Lawrence just a few kilometres downriver from
Île d'Orléans.

Between 1832 — the first year of the great cholera epidemics — and 1937, this island was the quarantine station for immigrants arriving from Europe. Ships loaded with hundreds of steerage passengers were inspected here and hospitals built to house the sick and dying. Thousands of victims of typhus and cholera are buried on Grosse Île; it is said that six thousand Irish immigrants perished here in 1847 alone.

Financing for quarantine facilities was uncertain, and the story of Grosse Île is a sad one. The first buildings were mere sheds, and the accounts of immigrants attempting to cleanse their possessions before being allowed to move on down the waterway to Upper Canada attest to primitive conditions and brutally unimaginative administration.

It's a ghost town now, containing twenty houses, shelters for fifteen hundred hospital beds, a church, a chapel, several empty shops — and acres and acres of graves. The federal quarantine station was moved to the St. Charles River in 1937, and the last use made of Grosse Île was as quarantine space for the importation of charolais cattle.

The Quebec Chamber of Commerce has thoughts of turning Grosse Île, along with several other St. Lawrence River islands, into a national park to commemorate the 450th anniversary, in 1984, of Jacques Cartier's famous first voyage. Alas, although the Department of Agriculture — which is now in charge of the island — is not against the plan, the place is protected by the Official Secrets Act; even flying over the island is forbidden. It is thought that it is being reserved by the Department of National Defence in case of bacteriological warfare.

During the nineteenth century several other islands were commandeered as lazarettos: Partridge Island outside Saint John, New Brunswick; Sheldrake near Newcastle; and McNabs Island outside Halifax. They too hold memories of despair and death. Those of us who search for our roots, as is now fashionable, ought to give a thought to those poor souls who, after long cramped voyages with poor food and bad water, arrived not at the promised land but in an unblessed and often communal island grave.

Île aux Coudres

Île aux Coudres is close to the northern bank of the St. Lawrence River near the town of Baie-Saint-Paul, about 90 kilometres northeast of Québec City. Like so many islands in the St. Lawrence, it was discovered by Jacques Cartier on his second voyage in 1535.

Québécois and Anglo carry completely different mental maps of Québec Province in their heads. Certain resorts on the north shore and certain lakes in the Eastern Townships are heaven to the Anglo. But if you ask a Québécois where to go, particularly if you are at the Festival of Baie-Saint-Paul, he'll point you to Île aux Coudres, the Isle of the Hazelnuts.

It's a small island and unprepossessing, except for a museum and the ruins of two great windmills, until you look into its history and realize that it is the heartland of old Québec. As Cartier sailed down the St. Lawrence with his fleet, the *Grande Hermine, Petite Hermine,* and *Émérillon,* the land became more and more possible, but the most accessible land took the form of islands, so it is of islands rather than of the shores beyond the high cliffs of the riverbank that we have the first description. Île aux Coudres he seized on at once in early September as a paradise of fruit and flowers; it was sheltered, the land looked good, and he wrote a glowing report on it.

Settlement proceeded slowly as it often did on Canadian islands, because back home in some European country the ownership papers were passing from hand to hand, but by 1651 there was a population of thirty. The British laid siege to it during the Seven Years War, and after the fall of Québec a few settlers came to add the name Hardy to the village rostrum. Meanwhile, the population grew and prospered, planting orchards and laying out fields of potatoes. There is good peat here, which is still bagged and sold to lovers of potted plants, and the early inhabitants also fished and went whaling and eeling, and hunting porpoises.

Most of all, however, Île aux Coudres is revered as the preserver of old Québec traditions. For a time, there was a thriving boat-building industry, and the old houses of the island go back to the finest traditions of the seventeenth century. Roadside crosses of great elegance are to be found along the coast; and I have been told, though have never seen it documented, that the first of the great furniture carvers of Québec settled here and that it was from Île aux Coudres that the artisans spread out to give Québec the artistic culture which none of the other provinces of the country can come up to.

"Everybody in Charlevoix County is called Tremblay," they told me in Baie-Saint-Paul, which was bannered and beautified for its festival, "and all the Tremblays came from the island." The old crafts persist, sometimes under the guidance of government-hired *animateurs culturels,* but the boat-building industry is coming to an end.

Sometimes the history of Québec has points of inaccessibility to those of us who were not brought up in the Catholic Church. I am on the whole unmoved by lists of parish priests and their dispositions on islands. I did, however, run across the story of one old curé with an immense and compulsory dislike of women, who after performing a marriage ceremony used to say, "Give me your six francs, take your beast, go."

A small population still remains to enjoy the fruit trees, the ruins of the great stone windmills, and the violent displays of Northern Lights which are the most sensational outside the Arctic. The people make music in the evening and talk about the old days when their whole lives were their boats. The old ways are not quite extinguished.

Anticosti Island

Anticosti, in the Gulf of St. Lawrence, is some 220 kilometres long — one of our larger islands. It is separated from Labrador by Jacques Cartier Strait and from the Gaspé Peninsula by the Strait of Honguedo.

The great grandeur of the trip down the St. Lawrence River is something we no longer routinely experience in these days of air travel. I was brought up on legends of this voyage—my father's eternal tale of returning to Canada after the 1914-18 War; and I sailed once in blazing autumn weather past Anticosti down to Sept-Îles and Baie-Comeau, greeted by the original weathered Shield decked in autumn grandeur, thinking, ''My God, do you mean I said I'd never come back to this?'' Jacques Cartier caught the excitement. He wrote that although the climate of Florida was probably more pleasant, there was nowhere to be found anything as beautiful as the landscape of Canada.

Anticosti was not the first island he found when he explored the Gulf of St. Lawrence in 1534; he seems to have said the first Mass in Canada on a good many different islands on the same day if you read enough local histories; but it was the largest. Mistaking its moose meadow for arable land, Louis Jolliet took it as his seigneury in 1680, along with the wind-sculpted Mingan Islands to the north. Partly because of an English invasion in 1690, but mostly because it was Anticosti and unprofitable, he abandoned it. It was eventually divided between his squabbling heirs and fell into a long history of historical disarray. By 1870, only 127 people were living here and it had a bad reputation for wreckers and piracy. It's referred to as the ''Cemetery of the Gulf,'' and the foggy channels around it are so difficult that 138 vessels were wrecked along its shores between 1828 and 1899. The wrecks were so bad and so frequent, and rescue so improbable, that the government established ''shipwreck stations'' along the coast, consisting of log cabins equipped with barrels of flour, peas, sugar, and coffee.

The wreck of the *Granicus* is the most famous in Anticosti lore. She sailed from Québec City for Cork on October 29, 1828, with a load of timber, a crew of twenty, and a number of passengers including three children and two women. She foundered between Fox Bay and East Point early in November and was too badly damaged to float again. The crew and passengers managed to rig up shelters on shore and survive the winter; when their food gave out in the spring, they rowed to Fox Bay to the government shelter: it was empty. The keeper, Olivier Godin, had abandoned it and taken away the food when his wife died that winter. The *Granicus* crew returned to their makeshift camp empty-handed.

On May 8 that year, the crew of a Magdalen Islands sealing schooner stopped to escape a storm and take on fresh water at the place where the *Granicus* people had camped. Accounts of what they found vary, but all are dramatic. They found a boat with stowed oars; a cabin; deathly silence. Near the cabin they found bloodstained women's and children's garments. Then, according to an affidavit they swore before a Justice of the Peace in the Magdalens on May 29, they ''found the door shut and tied inside with a rope . . .; on forcing the door they perceived the carcasses of four human beings with the heads, legs and arms cut off and the bowels extracted, hanging by the thighs in the room, and two others on the floor cut up . . .; that they found a human body in the hammock who appeared to have died there, the body was habited like a sailor; that there were two trunks in the room with human flesh in them cut up in small pieces, there was also a pot with human flesh in it and round the house pieces of human flesh and bones strewn about.''

Later, one of the sailors embroidered the tale by saying the man in the hammock was a mulatto, enormously tall, with huge shoulders, who had apparently died of indigestion.

Other investigations followed, and other accounts exist. A boat from Cape Breton recorded finding, farther down the coast, a board with the words written on it: "What sadness! What a pity!" Even seventy years later, chests containing human bones were dug up on the location. It's the most grisly of the Canadian shipwreck stories and no doubt encouraged the construction of the island's four lighthouses between 1831 and 1871.

In 1895, Henri Menier, the sportsman "Chocolate King of Europe" whose portraits resemble those of Edward VII and who had been searching for his own private island for some years, managed to buy Anticosti for $125,000 and bring it into a period of uncertain glory.

He and his agent, Georges Martin-Zédé, had dreams of colonization and empire, and seemingly unlimited funds. They brought in settlers, built a railway, established game reserves, banned dogs, and had trouble with a bunch of Methodist Newfoundlanders at Fox Bay. Although there were rumours that theirs was an effort by France to retake Canada, there is no doubt that to some extent the regime was intelligent and beneficial. For a time they minted their own coins and printed their own bank notes, but the Québec government did not allow them to make much use of this currency.

Menier built himself a grand house from which to play with his model society, and Martin-Zédé bustled around trying to make it profitable. Eventually, time and the pulp and paper industry overtook them; reluctantly, because they loved it, they sold the island that was bleeding them dry to the firm that became Consolidated-Bathurst.

When Anticosti proved unprofitable for traditional logging methods because of its odd geography (it's a stubborn island), the firm opened it as a game reserve for rich hunters; its deer and salmon were for a time the finest in the world, and its hotels $125 a night.

The Québec government bought the island in 1974 for some $25 million, and it is now a provincial park. Only about two hundred of the population remain, for the young men who worked in the mills and the logging camps have moved to Sept-Îles and to the big developments in Labrador. A good deal of Menier's seigneury still exists, however, and the islanders who remain are reported to be, like most islanders, intelligent, co-operative, and full of stories.

Prince Edward Island

This crescent-shaped island in the Gulf of St. Lawrence is Canada's smallest province, with an area of 5,657 square kilometres.

A curved raft of sandstone, it can obviously be shoved to the mainland in the mind, but because it is an island and a province as well, it is special and has its own flavour, its own ambience.

In the French period it was called Île Saint-Jean, and over two thousand souls had established themselves there before the British victory of 1759. It was heavily forested, but the first settlers found good red loam under the trees and good fishing grounds on the periphery. The long, slow wash of the tide mesmerized islanders: they are never disloyal to their place.

When Britain acquired Prince Edward Island, the Earl of Egmont wished to develop it in English-sounding "hundreds" (one always feels that Hobbits live in hundreds!) but the Colonial Office in London decided to divide it into three counties (Prince, Queens, and Kings, naturally) with three main towns, Princetown, Charlottetown, and Georgetown. Each town was to have one 66-acre plot — called a royalty reserve — as garden allotments for townsfolk. The rest of the island was then divided into sixty-seven 20,000-acre lots, of which one went to the crown and two to already established fish merchants, while the other sixty-four were handed out by lottery on July 23, 1767, to speculators and developers in Britain, many of them lords and younger sons.

The grantees were expected to settle one person per hundred acres, and these settlers were to be "foreign Protestants from the thirteen colonies and Europe." Land rents were to be two, four, or six shillings an acre, to be paid not by the grantees, one suspects, but by the farm tenants. That an Acadian community survived in the wooded northwest of the island is a tribute either to wiliness or to absent-minded absentee landlords.

Islanders sometimes today still speak of the ancient landlords, especially of the Hollands, whose tract was at Tryon. One of the Stuarts imported settlers from Argyll; thrifty Quakers were put down around New London; Loyalists moved in, Irish Protestants, and Highlanders from Skye. By 1805, 6057 souls inhabited Anne's Island, the ancestors of the feuding Methodists and Presbyterians that L. M. Montgomery described in her novels and tales a century later.

Prince Edward Island sounds like a Ruritanian dream, and in some ways it was and still is. Though the rents were rarely paid, though the pioneers suffered severely from isolation and frost, and though the shipbuilding industry that made P.E.I. a feature of the Maritime Museum in Greenwich, England, foundered and failed like its ships, Prince Edward Island is a place many of us head for in summer with purest affection.

My generation knows it almost with embarrassment because of our love of the sentimental novels of Lucy Maud Montgomery, the clever orphan who thought she could write her way out of personal disaster, like the rest of us found she couldn't, and went on writing anyway. Her Anne is a figure who stays in the mind, red-headed, volatile, a fourteen-year-old tartar who grows up to be what she longs to be, a mother of seven.

Montgomery was also the perpetrator of a heroine named Emily who wanted to be a writer and was in love with a man named Dean Priest, and of one named Kilmeny who thought she was ugly because her mother forbade mirrors and she could only look at herself in spoons. In short, Montgomery was a turn-of-the-century romantic of a sort to make a modern feminist blush. When I was ten or twelve I adored her; I even remember the covers of her books — puce, in the Boston edition, with pasted-on women's portraits — and some of the endings.

Recent biographers have discovered that Montgomery's life was anything but a bed of roses; having been dominated by a neurotic grandmother, she married and was dominated by a neurotic clergyman-husband; she looked not into the heart of her own condition but back to the magical landscape, and created magical fictional lives with all sordidness removed. Her best work was her first, *Anne of Green Gables*, and has contributed enormously to the island tourist industry. You can go and have a good cry over Matthew's death every summer at the Confederation Theatre, visit the house that has been designated Green Gables, and golf next door to it.

Prince Edward Island is very beautiful, the colour of my red cat gliding through green grass in summer. It looks peaceful: potato fields lined up and numbered for the airplane sprayers, low, soft tidal flats, thickets of spruce and pine and wild roses, white houses beautifully painted, white churches that are their own denominational dreams.

We stayed one summer in a friend's house at Cape Traverse, once a large village whence iceboats had set out in winter for Cape Tormentine, New Brunswick. (Incredibly brave men used to shove you across the channel, clambering aboard when the ice broke before they went through. The local doctor sold kittens of gin to the wisest passengers, and the bottles are collectors' items now.) When the ferry port was opened at Borden, eight kilometres away, most of the houses of Cape Traverse were moved there. Of the seven houses that remained I managed to occupy, that summer, two; I got to know the place a little and move out of the sweet Green Gables dream.

I used to talk to Claude as he raked his Irish moss out to dry on the road. He said they sold their lobsters for a nickel a pound during the Depression, just to keep their kids alive. Later, they'd go up to Ontario to work in factories in the winter and come back to the good life — a little lobstering, a little moss — in the summer. I used to talk to Grace, who bought her house from an ad in the paper when she discovered she was going to be left alone with four babies for three years on an army base in Edmonton. "Sight unseen," she said. "The army would move you to an owned house but not a rented one, so I subscribed to all the Maritime papers, picked this one out from an ad, and put the down payment on it from what I'd saved out of the baby bonus." We'd sit and speculate about whether Montgomery might have been better off marrying her semi-literate childhood sweetheart, and Grace would tell me how it was funny on the island, the real aristocracy was measured by the number of acres of potatoes they had.

But it's hard in summer to get a real measure of a place, especially one that's blooming with roses and lupins, and crammed with tourists. In winter, with the wind shrieking in from the gulf, there are the same pinched faces as everywhere, the toy-village look gives over to reality, and you know there aren't many jobs and there isn't much cheap land to be had. Georgetown has a large, empty port — big enough for deep-sea vessels with only a few lobster pots on the quay — and everyone was more concerned to get the McDonald's French-fry concession than to re-open the gem of a theatre there.

Whenever I'm back there in summer — I walk into the green gloom of Hilda's kitchen which the plants took over years ago, and the dogs Scott and Kaye look up and nod wisely, and the kids come down and say, ''You're back again'' — I dream of moving down; but something always stops me; it's someone else's dream of a place, not mine, because, I think, more than any other province of Canada, P.E.I. escaped the Industrial Revolution, and I simply feel better when I'm close to the foundries and railway tracks I grew up among.

No major industry has survived long on the island. There's a Canadian Armed Forces base at Summerside, there's the eternal parade of tourists, there's the fishing industry; but the ship-building is long gone, and they cut down the sugar bush for a hydro right-of-way last year: none of my Ontario landmarks exist.

The economy has been depressed for a long time; the hope for P.E.I. is that it is going to leap from the eighteenth to the twenty-first century, for there are thriving arts and crafts projects, a good educational system, some of the most interesting experiments I've seen in solar technology, and moves to bring in government departments to make up for the lack of industry. More than in any other part of Canada, one feels in Prince Edward Island that intelligence is directed not to a sentimental past for reasons of tourism but towards a possible, the only possible, future. For this province, without its own energy supplies, without an industrial base, has still to make its way; and perhaps, because it is not inhibited by its past, it will do so.

Meanwhile, there are the quarrels about development in Charlottetown, what to teach at the university, whether or not the realistic painters are the best. There are parties with folk songs and step-dancing and rhubarb wine. Lobster suppers and mussels from New London. Dreaming shores again, where once I watched a small insomniac boy build a whole world under a full moon on a red-sand tidal beach. Perhaps it's all right once in a while to leave sordid reality behind and think only about the good things.

The Magdalen Islands/
Îles de la Madeleine

An archipelago of a dozen islands, seven of which are inhabited, the Magdalens are in the Gulf of St. Lawrence, about 110 kilometres to the northeast of Prince Edward Island, and are part of the Province of Québec. They are connected to one another by sand dunes and rocks.

Once they were mountaintops, and of all the islands I have been to they are perhaps the most mixed up and the most magical. They are a confusion of long white beaches where you can still beachcomb shipwrecks, red rocks honeycombed with caves, and haunted heronries and lagoons.

They were discovered, of course, by our old friend Jacques Cartier, though they share the ambulatory history of most of the East Coast and must have been temporary havens for fishermen from the time of the Vikings on. They were leased in 1653 to Nicolas Denys by the Company of a Hundred Associates. The first organized walrus hunt was held there in 1706 and, as we know, the seal hunt still goes on. Meanwhile, a mixed population of shipwrecked English sailors, French immigrants, expelled Acadians, and Miquelonnais who wished to escape the French Revolution began to form a population known as "Madelinots." Québec folklore has it that it is here that the pure Acadian type still survives: the impressively tall *grand gaillard*.

By the Québec Act of 1774, the Magdalens became part of Lower Canada. They were the most isolated and uncontrollable part of the province, and Lord Dorchester settled them on Captain Isaac Coffin of the Royal Marines on condition that the town of Old Harry on Grosse Île become a Protestant clergy reserve.

Coffin is not a popular name in the Magdalens. He charged the settlers twenty sous an acre for the rent of lands which they thought they already owned and went on, through his descendants, collecting these rents until the 1940s. He brought in English settlers, changed place names around, and created a schizophrenia on the islands that is still hard to sort out.

You can go there by air or by the ferry *Lucy Maud Montgomery* from Souris, Prince Edward Island, and you are encouraged by the Québec government to do so because a failing fishery is being replaced by tourism. Having passed the English settlement of Entry Island, where the lighthouse is, you arrive at a town known as Grindstone/Cap-aux-Meules that seems at first as gritty as its name. The usual high banks covered with Irving oil tanks around the harbour; the usual scattering of stores and gas stations and restaurants around the cove. I stayed there once in a looming old hotel, where the woodwork had all been grained with a varnish-comb and not a doily had been replaced except to wash it since 1935, and played a game called The Minister's Cat with my two kids, who were recovering from seasickness all night. Next day I talked to two wonderful old women who had come from Entry Island for a checkup at the hospital. "It's all French here," they said sadly, "but on Entry, now, we're as English as they come."

The large islands, Cap aux Meules, Havre Aubert (Amherst Island), Havre aux Maisons, Grosse Île, Île de l'Ést, and Grande Entrée, are joined by long, dreaming sand dunes where there are not red rocks. The farms lie inland and, from the road, you do not see many of the canvas-capped haystacks that make the place agriculturally famous. Rather, French villages with their houses close to the road like birds on a wire, and English villages standing back in clerical reserve. I hitchhiked the length of these islands one summer with my two kids to see a friend of ours called Farley Mowat, who then lived at the very end of the very last road on a gorgeous promontory.

I remember only two pieces of the dinner conversation: "Well, kids, if you don't like mackerel, by all means eat peanut butter: there's no fish around at all this summer" and "Have you got fifty bucks, Marian? Glenna's cottage is empty this week. Claire and I used to go there before we built this place: you'll love it."

My protests that Bill and Charlotte ought not to miss the beginning of school were overruled and we found ourselves in a little house in Old Harry, from which we could go to a red beach by climbing down a big frayed rope or to a white beach by walking less than a kilometre, or reach the inner lagoons of Old Harry Bay by exerting ourselves on a path through the sedge. Our landlady, Glenna, showed us what washed-up walrus teeth looked like, and we paddled along between high tide and low, jealously guarding our finds from each other. It was too cold to swim so I didn't even have to lifeguard. The children played all day on the marvellous strands, waving to curious seals who bobbed up to see who we were. Bill scaled a tiny island offshore and stood waving from its green crest, king of the world. When we souped happily along the roads and lagoons, I held fast to my bird book, counting shorebirds I had never seen before, especially my first avocets.

On the Sunday, a vehicle arrived at our door and transported us to a dock for a picnic. Mowat's boat looked to me like all the marines landing at once, but the children had no fear of it and were thrilled to take the wheel. We landed on Seal Island in Old Harry lagoon and had our lunch on curious, dry, spongy turf that had been fertilized by centuries of bird droppings, for the place was a heronry. The children looked down into rat holes and, with Farley, began to dig. Treasure! Walrus bones! They still lie around our house — pelvises, I suppose, and shoulder blades, old and brown, for the last walruses were killed for their blubber and ivory in the eighteenth century.

The fishery in the Gulf of St. Lawrence may have improved, but that year it was in bad shape, and many fishermen were living on welfare and garden produce until the sealing should start in the winter. The Mowat house, being at the end of the very last road, became the final stop on the route of the tour buses which the government was encouraging as local industry; it is impossible to write when your doorbell rings constantly, so the Mowats have left. The lagoons have been changed because of the erection of an experimental wind-power project for the islands.

I'd like to return to the Magdalens and explore the shipwreck coast on the west beach which joins Grindstone to Amherst Island (to give them their English names). I won't recapture that magic summer, for the kids are too old now to play The Minister's Cat all night and spend whole days flinging sand at each other from behind shale redoubts; but we were talking about the Magdalens the other day and have not lost the feeling we got of the mystery of the walrus lagoons and the majesty of heron-shadows over our summer heads.

Nova Scotian Islands

The shores of Nova Scotia are as fiorded as those of Newfoundland, and there seems to be no reason why large island populations did not spring up and remain as they did on Newfoundland's Change Islands and Fogo and Twillingate. Even Cape Sable, Long Island, Brier Island, and the Tusket Islands — the largest along the south and west coasts of the Nova Scotian peninsula — have not thrown up any great body of lore. They are, on the other hand, very beautiful islands, and they and their smaller brethren have become so attractive to outsiders that there are two brokers in the Mahone Bay area who deal in islands alone.

Brier Island, which after Long Island is the farthest extension of that wonderful peninsula Digby Neck, was the home of that famous old salt Joshua Slocum, whose *Sailing Alone Around the World* remains a classic of seadog lore. I still can't look at the map of South America without thinking of old Slocum putting carpet tacks on the deck of his boat to keep the wild natives of Tierra del Fuego from attacking: much better than Darwin's account.

Oak Island in Mahone Bay has for generations been a Mecca for a certain sort of adventurer whose mother told him too often that a fool and his money are soon parted. Here, legend has it, Captain Kidd buried his treasure, and here every sort of entrepreneur, from CBC producers on up, comes to dig. Elaborate schemes are invested in; walls cave in; workmen drown in excavations that have found the water table rather than gold; persistence has, as far as I know, never been rewarded, but the search goes on.

Mahone Bay and its neighbour St. Margarets — in fact the whole Nova Scotia shore from Peggy's Cove to Lunenburg and Blue Rocks — is one of the most beautiful stretches of country in Canada and one of the most civilized. The islands of both bays are studded with gems of white summer houses (perhaps some of them were once residences of shipbuilding and shipping kings in Nova Scotia's grand wooden-ship days) and along the shores there are excellent inns and seafood restaurants.

It's bitter country in winter — the season that separates the men from the boys on most Canadian islands — but brilliant summers and a renewed boat-building industry at Chester have made it a deservedly popular resort area. Perhaps it is the fact that the hinterland of these islands is so attractive that accounts for one's few opportunities to visit them.

The most famous island off the Nova Scotia coast is, of course, Sable Island, "the Graveyard of the Atlantic," a thirty-kilometre shifting crescent of dune and beach that has accounted for two hundred shipwrecks in the past hundred and seventy years and is still regarded as a major navigational hazard.

Sable lies southeast of Halifax at 43°57′ N and 59°55′ W, a designation probably well known to all mariners. In the past, there have been five different life-saving stations there; these were abandoned in 1948. Now Sable Island is home to a meteorology station; and it's the breeding place of the Ipswich sparrow and several rare kinds of gull, and famous of course for its wild ponies, descendants of many Maritime shipwrecks. Sadly, the ponies have been exported from time to time for dog food, and there are winters when not many survive, even though hay is airlifted to them. Their perfect peace is also threatened by that almost universal East Coast threat, the offshore oil rig.

Sable is being progressively consumed by the sea; its lighthouses have constantly crumbled and had to be replaced by new structures farther inland. In time, the sandy crescent may turn into a tiny shoal sheltering a few lost ponies and the lonely survivor of a drowned oil rig.

Cape Breton Island

Now part of the province of Nova Scotia and joined to it by a causeway, Cape Breton was formerly a French stronghold, guarding the entrance to the Gulf of St. Lawrence and threatening the British presence on the Nova Scotian mainland.

The high green shoulders of Cape Breton Island stand proudly in the sea on a fine day. It's a big island with a wild past and a wild climate, and its main highway is also a famous tourist artery — the Cabot Trail, which winds nearly 500 kilometres over mountain and dale, through settlements which were often bilingual in Gaelic and French before the arrival of television.

The undulating land mass of Precambrian rock, heavily indented and thrusting northeast into the Atlantic Ocean, was a source of coal to the steel industry at Sydney for many years, and pathetic accounts are still told of accidents in mine shafts which reach far beyond the land mass under the sea. The iron industry in the Sydney-Glace Bay industrial area has been in trouble for some time, but there is always hope of reconstruction there.

Highland settlements in the eastern part of Cape Breton were for many years isolated and picturesque. Alexander Graham Bell had a summer home at Baddeck, where he mounted the first recorded flight in the British Empire with an engine-powered kite. There is a museum in the old resort town now.

The French presence on Cape Breton was strongly established in the early 1720s, when construction of a grand fort at Louisbourg was begun. It was an ambitious project, and for the thirty-odd years before it was destroyed by the British in 1758 the fort was a centre of commerce and military deployment in the area.

Although I learned in Europe to be cynical about restorations, which often say more about the restorers' times than the original era, I can't find it in my heart even to wonder whether the Louisbourg reconstruction is authentic. Begun in 1961, it is now quite wonderful, a classic piece of fortification encompassing a small city. It has good restaurants and interesting craft shops, and bids fair to compete well with Williamsburg. It can be reached by bus from Sydney.

Even when mines and smelters are closed, Sydney maintains its dignity as a trade centre. It has Cape Breton's major airport, and the ferries that connect Nova Scotia and Port-aux-Basques, Newfoundland, carry large amounts of freight to both the tenth province and the smaller islands of the Gulf of St. Lawrence. There's a tough Glasgow liveliness here, for all that we think of Cape Breton as a rural paradise.

It's beautiful, this island, and interesting in its mixture of Acadian and Scottish settlements gracing the ringing valleys and lochs. It's no closer to paradise, however, than any other Canadian island. There is land to be farmed, but the summers are short. The fishing fleets do not create millionaires. To those of us who live in kinder environments, the miners' stories are horror stories. Summer visitors who stream up and down the trail, wearing Nova Scotia tartan ties and buying lobster pots to strap on their ski-racks, are now a necessary part of the island's economy, and what they get as they plunder the plangent landscape for visual treasure is a perception of highland, sea, and mountain, of rough landscape and tough living redeemed by hard work, which is deeply satisfying to the puritanical soul of North America.

Île de la Demoiselle

Off the Labrador coast, in that part of the Gulf of St. Lawrence which leads into the Strait of Belle Isle, lies a small island which is seldom marked in atlases but which has given rise to the most romantic Canadian island stories I have ever heard. It is part of an archipelago called Îles du Vieux Fort, where some three hundred trappers and fishermen still eke out an existence, and it is probably the island which was once known as Île aux Démons.

Jean François de la Rocque, Sieur de Roberval, was, following Jacques Cartier's revelation of the value of the territory, made viceroy of New France, and in 1542 he put together an expedition to his new kingdom. He was not a man of good temper or good luck, and few of his ventures were successful.

He took his niece Marguerite along with him, and others of his family, but when they reached the Labrador coast it was revealed to him that she had been having a love affair with one of the young cavaliers of his party. He summarily chose an island, put Marguerite and her nurse Damienne, some meagre supplies, and four "arquebuses" in a small boat and sent it ashore. Her lover jumped off the larger vessel and swam to join them. Roberval sailed on to lose most of his party to scurvy that winter when he camped near the future site of Québec.

Two years and five months later, a shipload of fishermen passing the island saw smoke coming from a primitive habitation and had the courage to stop and track down the legend of a ghostly presence on this island, which was by now called Île aux Démons. They found Marguerite dressed all in furs and rags, alone and half savage. Her nurse had died, her lover had died, even her baby had died. She had lived on alone, tending her fire, and for food and clothing shooting white bears with her ancient musket. She had, she said, been half frightened out of her wits by the painted savages. (Were they the last of the Beothuks?) One wonders what the savages thought of her.

The fishermen took her back to France, but she found it politic to hide in the Périgord until Roberval died about fifteen years later. One hopes that she lived to a grand old age, gorging herself on goose liver, walnuts, and good claret.

Island Bird Sanctuaries

Many islands in the Gulf of St. Lawrence and off the coast of Newfoundland have been designated as bird sanctuaries, for they are breeding places for gannets, puffins, gulls, murres, cormorants, and many other varieties of sea birds.

One of the most interesting is Bird Rock, which lies between the north point of the Magdalens and Newfoundland, and is famous not only for its magnificent birds but for its life-saving lighthouse, erected in 1860, a great feat of engineering considering that the sides of the rock are almost vertical.

Bonaventure Island, off the Gaspé coast near Percé; Great, Gull, and Green islands, east of Newfoundland's Avalon Peninsula (not to be confused with other Gull and Green islands in Newfoundland); and Cape St. Mary's, between Placentia Bay and St. Mary's Bay on the south coast of Newfoundland, are also sanctuaries.

The most remote of the sanctuaries of the Gulf of St. Lawrence is on the Funk Islands (from *Funk: obs. A strong smell or stink:* OED) out in the Atlantic a bit farther than the gulf really extends, fifty kilometres east of Fogo Island. The Funks can be approached with difficulty and at great expense, and in good weather only. Franklin Russell, in his marvellous book *The Secret Islands*, describes standing on the Funks amongst murderously quarrelsome murres, kittiwakes, and puffins, and thinking himself back to the Battle of Culloden. He was astounded to find himself walking among the bones of great auks, which have been extinct for a hundred and fifty years. Not a tourist voyage.

Fogo Island

Fogo is the largest island off the northeastern coast of Newfoundland. It lies in Notre Dame Bay, which is close to the cod banks and includes many famous outports and famous names: Dildo Run, New World Island, the Change Islands, and such islands as Exploits, Triton, Pilley's, Thwart, Dunnage, Twillingate, Bacalhao, and Sunday Cove. Here's where the men set out for the northern part of the seal hunt and where death is a next-door neighbour.

Those of the peripheral islands of Newfoundland which are still inhabited are working islands — there's no resort quality to them as there is in the warmer islands of the Great Lakes and the British Columbian coast. And where arts and crafts thrive, it's because the women still prefer to knit their fishermen-husbands' two-fingered mittens from their own sheep-shearings, though they send them to St. John's now to be spun.

You arrive on Fogo by a ferry that rolls across Hamilton Sound to Seldom Come By. We hitchhiked to the motel that lies at the interior crossroads by the schoolhouse, the new high school, and the library; as it was Saturday night, I went with some trepidation into the adjoining pub to see if I could get a line on a place to stay by the seaside. It was dark, and the faces of the men were backlit by the light of the bar. For a moment I thought I was in an old Barry Fitzgerald movie. I sat down at a table with a young couple, though I'd have been inclined to sit alone if there'd been a free space. The band blared country-western, lonely songs about what it was like to have a man at sea. I stared at the people; the women looked tired and rather ordinary, but the men in the half-light had these faces from movies, and a man nearby looked astonishingly like Shakespeare. The man at my table told me he was home for the summer from Toronto, a lot of them were. His girl talked to me in a low voice that I couldn't discern over the band, but her accent was soft and Irish.

I said what I was doing, probably shouted it over the music, and Shakespeare said, ''Look, my mother runs the youth hostel in Tilting Harbour; she'd be glad to have you.''

It was what is called falling on your feet. We got a ride next morning to Tilting with the Fogo taxi driver, who informed us as we were passing through Joe Batt's Arm that Captain Cook had married a woman from there. (Joe Batt, I later learned, was a deserter from Captain Cook's survey ship; perhaps that was the reason for the myth about Cook's wife, who was in fact an English girl). We went through Barr'd Islands and Sandy Cove as well before we got to Tilting and eventually found the hostel, a small fish store painted with yellow flowers.

The owner and my daughter and I took to each other at once; I was immediately installed in the hostel, a simple upstairs room reached by a ladder, which contained any writer's real essentials: a bed with a patchwork quilt, a hooked rug, a table and chair, an oil lamp and view. Mrs. Ryan said Charlotte could sleep at the house if she wanted, she'd like a room of her own.

Then we went out for a walk, up over the cliffs behind the house; from there we could see Pigeon Island (for in Newfoundland every island has an island, as every cat has seven kits) and the Little Fogos twinkling in the sunshine, and the sailboats going out there for their special summer Sunday church service.

Most of Newfoundland tends to be bare bedrock, and what's laid over it is squashy turf that reminds one of northern Ontario moose meadow. We leapt from hummock to hummock behind our athletic hostess, who, though she'd raised her children in Toronto mostly, had been born in Tilting and known the drier parts of the paths all her life. We saw no pitcher plants, but the land was studded with runty irises, blue as sapphires. Sheep graze free on Fogo and we had to keep the dog from chasing them onto the rocks, except in one case where a newly weaned lamb was hopefully chasing the big white dog.

"There's where the boys used to swim," Mrs. Ryan said, "and there's where the girls used to swim. We never went together in those days. Let's go on up there and see if the bake apples are ready yet." These are what the Scots call cloudberries, and they look like raspberries in a whorl of wintergreen leaves. In this underendowed, windswept territory, they're a valuable source of vitamin C. Mrs. Ryan taught us how to snap them off to avoid tearing them up by the roots.

Then we walked down by the allotment gardens, all neatly picketed with the trunks of the stunted spruce of the island, and talked to the people who were out cultivating their potatoes and turnips on such a fine day. Finally, passing wandering cattle and horses and chickens, we circled back along the paved village road to the house for a tea of chicken and cheese, homemade jam, and a little moosemeat so we could see how well they lived there.

They do, in their own way. Fogo is one of the communities that refused Joey Smallwood's offer to drag it kicking and screaming into the twentieth century. Some residents were tempted by the great move, but most, whose ancestors had begun to come here from Ireland and Scotland in 1680, became active in the Island Improvement Committee and participated in a local-consciousness movement inspired by the extension service of Memorial University in St. John's. They knew there were still enough cod and seal on the northern banks to keep them and decided not to be moved. Instead, they formed a co-operative to market their fish and turned themselves into a go-ahead community.

Mind you, it wouldn't look go-ahead to a man from New York. In Tilting, although the water table is high, the ground underneath the houses is bare rock; therefore not all of the houses have running water. People hire a boy or send one of their own children to the standpipe to fetch the water home in buckets, wearing a metal carrying-frame. It took me a couple of days to take in the fact that the Enclosure Act hasn't happened here; the animals graze free and the gardens are fenced in; that's why I awoke one morning to a strange snuffling and found four horses staring up to my window, echoing my mellifluous snoring. They are not much used in the summer, but sledges left along the road indicate that they haul wood out of the bush in the winter.

The fishing is still good: the neighbour next door hauled up 600 kilograms of cod one morning while I was there. In the sunset one evening I saw a curious sight: men standing in boats against a red sky, looking like the figures in Millet's *The Angelus*, praying. "Ha!" Mrs. Ryan laughed. "We're Catholic, but not that Catholic. They're jigging squid."

That night, writing by lamplight for the first time since I was a child (in a similar room, in the farmhouse where my mother was born in Ontario), I put down: "In Toronto you can hide away from the weather; anyway, it's collective: when your basement floods, so do a thousand others, and the city takes care of you. Here, every house sticks out into the weather, unprotected by rows of others; even your shelter isn't sheltered. There's nothing between you and Tobermory in Scotland when your hat blows away. It's warmer outside than in when it rains, as it is in England, and the rain is wetter, and they say that in the winter you can't go out for the wind sometimes, and from the size of the vegetation I believe them."

Tilting is the prettiest outport on Fogo. We went through Joe Batt's and Barr'd Islands again to see Fogo town and the few grand merchants' houses, built in the days when English companies, particularly from Dorset, controlled the fish trade. They were bought out eventually by companies from St. John's. Now they tend to be replaced by co-ops. People still say "the merchants" with a certain bitterness.

It's a good life on Fogo for active men; they fish in summer, sometimes go sealing ("swiling") in winter, though they weren't talking about that, and go off into the bush to get caribou or moose to put in the freezer. The women, I suspect, have a thinner time of it, depending on whether they like housework or not. On fine days there is a general rush to fill clothes lines and picket fences with laundry. The old people tend to leave because there's only a cottage hospital to deal with their physical problems. But those who still live on Fogo are there because they love it, and since the co-op came the welfare payments on the island have been reduced by sixty per cent.

On the cliffs in summer, blue irises wink at the sun and woolly sheep run and bleat. The best trout ponds in the world are here, and there are salmon in the rivers, lobsters in the harbour. Not a bad place in good weather.

Newfoundland

Canada's fourth largest island (the other three are Baffin, Victoria, and Ellesmere, all in the Arctic), Newfoundland is also our most eastern province, washed on three sides by the Atlantic Ocean.

Too large an island for the scope of this book perhaps, but there are things to be said about it all the same, for it is still, to a large number of us, unknown territory. We hear about the oil rights, we sing its folk songs and tell Newfie jokes, but because it did not become part of Canada until 1949 we are still largely ignorant of its history, which is fascinating.

It's the closest part of Canada to Europe, and carbon-dating has established that there was a Viking settlement at Anse-aux-Meadows in 1000 A.D. We were told in school that it was discovered by John Cabot in 1497, but evidence suggests that Norsemen, Basques, and other Europeans had been whaling and walrusing and fishing in Newfoundland waters long before. The high sheer cliffs of Labrador, the northern islands of Newfoundland, and the excellent ports of the south were no strangers to itinerant European ships. Even after the English claimed the island, fishing rights along the western "French shore" were assigned to France. History must go back far beyond the history we are officially taught.

Settlement in Newfoundland and Labrador was not encouraged until the early eighteenth century because of the cost of maintaining people over the long, sterile winter. The rough north coasts have, however, been home to a scattered population, very poor and very tough, who were referred to in early chronicles and colloquially as "livyers"; because, as opposed to the majority in the Labrador fishery, they lived here all year round. According to some sources, they were of fugitive Acadian stock; others regard them to have originated with the employees of the British merchant firms who ruled the fisheries in the early 1800s.

Chances are that anyone whose ancestors were livyers — surviving from summer fishing and winter trapping — has been toughened by a mixture of Inuit, Basque, French, or Montagnais Indian stock and by a great experience of islands and icebergs.

Southern Newfoundland has a more decorous history; people's tendency to stay put enables social geographers to trace whole communities back to depressed villages in Dorset and Devon and the south of Ireland, eager to find jobs for their young men. Newfoundland's architecture has something in common with that of the East Coast from Boston on up through Halifax and Charlottetown — frame houses of a grand period — but, in the outports, typical styles have sprung up and are now being preserved.

What those of us who have not much travelled in Newfoundland fail to realize from looking at it on the map is that it is huge and that they're not fooling when they call it "the Rock." Cliffsides fall from great heights into the water and only a thin layer of muskeg covers much of the land. I travelled down the beautiful, empty Burin Peninsula with a Japanese geographer who was amazed at all the empty land. I was as well, until I tried to think how to populate it. The sheep would get foot-rot; you'd have to put stockfish in all those twinkling shallow ponds which make you think the French are geniuses for calling their puddles *flaques*; and the populace would get consumption from living in the damp. Farther inland there is indeed some arable land, but on the whole Newfoundland is all coast and no hinterland, not much of an economic proposition if the oil spoils the fishery.

The last Beothuk Indian in Newfoundland is said to have died on Triton Island in 1829, though there are other accounts and the *National Atlas of Canada* shows a scattering of Micmac here and there. It's the one province of Canada, however, where the Indian presence is scarcely visible — and the only one where I've heard people boast of having Indian blood.

What's exciting about Newfoundland now, besides the coming of the oil industry and the squabble over rights, is the number of artists who are springing up to tell its story. Harold Horwood's books are the best known I suppose, but a league of poets and playwrights are following in his footsteps and there are wonderful artists, like David Blackwood and Mary and Christopher Pratt: in fact, a whole school of them down near Ferryland where the Masterless Men used to run wild.

And why not? It's as big as Ireland and as much an entity unto itself. It's a place where they still make their own music and their own beer, perhaps the only place in Canada outside Québec where there's that combination of homogeneity and isolation that causes what we call a culture to spring up.

St. John's has a steep-sided harbour, garnished with oil-storage tanks, and port facilities that are the oldest and most cosmopolitan in North America. Currently, it's suffering from a shortage of hotel rooms caused by the oil boom. The local accent, at least among taxi drivers, is heavily Irish; the hardware stores are more like ship chandlers' warehouses than the Woolworth's ours have tended to become. There's a grittiness about the city: it verges on the picturesque and emerges into the utilitarian. The merchants are still grimly there for business rather than for pleasure; the Marconi monument dominates the town from the fortifications above the Battery Hotel, and I suspect that the inner workings of the place are as complicated as a clock's.

St. John's has modern suburbs now, but a good deal of the population commutes from the nearer outports like Beachy Cove and Portugal Cove in Conception Bay, and Bay Bulls and Petty Harbour on the gulf coast of the Avalon Peninsula. Although the iron mines are shut down, Bell Island is still alive and the people who live there swear by its stony attractions.

The thirties were dirtier in Newfoundland than anywhere else in North America. It was still a British colony, and because of mismanagement and political scandals, its legislative assembly had been cancelled; it was being run from Britain as a kind of transatlantic soup kitchen, and the population suffered terribly from low prices for fish, agricultural failures, and industrial depression. They drew, like members of a proud, impoverished family, closer together than the rest of us.

It's important not to sentimentalize their poverty — it may still look picturesque, but it was in our own time horrendous. A friend of mine whose father was a doctor remembers his being paid in braces of duck and handsome knit mittens, sometimes years after the account was closed. I met a man who was one of twenty-five children in an inland family and he said that the ones that went to school were the ones who got out of bed first and scrabbled into a pair of shoes. The barefoot went into the bush, and since there was never room to sit at table together, nobody knew who was gone and there wasn't time to care.

It's a good life in a good year, in Newfoundland, and there are songs to sing, but a certain obstreperousness is built into the character and it's going to be interesting to watch the island's political future. Prosperity is bound to produce an interesting reaction.

The Call of the Islands

Somewhere at this very moment a ferry is pulling out from a dock and setting off for an island. The mainland will recede with its complicated facilities; the shore of the island will advance, promising simplicity (to those who can dismantle electric pumps) and a change, at least for a while, of lifestyle.

I will not be on that ferry as it chugs or rumbles across sound, river, strait, lake, or fiord. Nor will I be on any of the numerous mosquito-sized airplanes which deposit city folks on islands in the summer. I shall be tied to the mast, resisting the siren call of pebbled and sandy shores, telling myself that I have to do something different because I've seen all the islands.

I haven't, of course, but I'm staying away from islands, resisting the lure of ferries. You can call me up and tell me you're going to the one where the grass-of-Parnassus grows, or the fringed gentians, or that you've found a super ruin that you think you can attribute to yet another European with delusions of Empire, and I'll just say that I think I really ought to change the subject and stay home. I've got to get some work done before my junket to Manitoulin takes place, and then I have to figure out if I can afford to go back to Fogo and. . . .

Of all diseases, islomania is the least curable and the most enjoyable.

Opposite: The westernmost group of islands in Canada, the Queen Charlottes are endowed with fabulous rain forests, the best of which will soon all be logged and gone unless steps are taken to preserve them.

Opposite: The sisters Sherri Lightbown and
Sunni Beynon model the blankets they have
made, in front of the longhouse at Haida,
Queen Charlotte Islands.

Above: Gwaii Edenshaw of Masset, British
Columbia. In the Haida language, his name
means ''Island.''

Above left: Harold Yeltatzie sculpts a killer
whale in his home in Masset, Queen Charlotte
Islands. Inlaid with abalone shell, the carving
is made from argillite, a rare slate available
only to the Haida people.

Above right: Matriarch of an artistic family,
Florence Davidson relaxes in her home in
Haida, Queen Charlotte Islands. Behind her
hangs a banner designed by her famous
grandson Robert Davidson.

Opposite: The work of Alfie Collinson of
Skidegate, Queen Charlotte Islands, is highly
prized by museums and astute collectors. His
new carving studio gives evidence of his
extraordinary talent.

Opposite: Most graveyards are located in clearings; the settler's cemetery outside Masset on the Queen Charlotte Islands is unusual in its forest setting.

Above: Totems and a lone cross in the Nimkish burial grounds at Alert Bay on Cormorant Island, British Columbia.

Above: Self-sufficient homesteaders, Fran and
Steve Morrow and Fran's brother Dennis
Seidemann, live on Porcher Island,
British Columbia.

Opposite: The forest grows over the ruins of a
logging truck at Gillies Bay on Texada Island,
British Columbia.

Above: Author, pilot, sailor, musician, and wood craftsman, among other things, Bo Curtis earns his living as a lightkeeper. Here he touches up the foghorns of Scarlett Point on Balaklava Island in British Columbia.

Opposite: The end of a long day at Balaklava Island is not the end of work for the keeper, who will be getting up several times during the night to check the weather. The highline silhouetted above the work shed is used to haul up supplies brought in by ship, such as the piano played by the keeper's wife.

Above: Ross Fuoco makes a stained-glass
lampshade in his workshop at Quathiaski Cove
on Quadra Island, British Columbia. On the
wall in front of him is a sketch of his design
for the window of a local church at nearby
Cape Mudge Village.

Opposite: Carol and Richard Martin's back
porch is part of an attractive hand-built home,
one of many on Hornby Island which benefit
from an absence of restrictive codes and the
mild climate of coastal British Columbia.

Above: Alan Steward of Mayne Island raises cattle rather than the sheep more commonly seen in the Gulf Islands of British Columbia.

Opposite: Wayne Ngan, one of Canada's very best potters, stands at the entrance to his studio on Hornby Island. A consummate craftsman, everything he makes looks like a work of art, even the outdoor privy in the woods behind the studio.

Overleaf: Low tide in the Gulf Islands reveals large numbers of starfish. The British Columbia coast supports the greatest variety of starfish in the world.

Above: This detail on Galiano Island, British
Columbia, is part of a beach consisting
entirely of bits of sea shells.

Opposite: Sunset from Galiano Island outlines the
mountains of Vancouver Island across one of
the passageways of the Strait of Georgia.

Opposite: Strange, eroded forms are common along the sandstone shores of British Columbia's Gulf Islands.

Above: The late afternoon sun illuminates an arbutus tree overhanging the cliffed shore of northern Galiano Island.

Above: In her eighties, Elizabeth Hopkins on Galiano Island has become a recognized and respected painter since checking out of an old folks' home some years ago.

Opposite: Following centuries-old designs, Gregory Foster of Galiano Island builds boats meant for sail power only. Beginning with nothing more refined than salvaged logs cast adrift from booms, and working with a minimum of tools, his skilled hands have created numerous elegant vessels, such as this *Isle of Shoals* model.

Above: Dorothy and Neptune Navy Grimmer
of Pender Island, British Columbia. An
accomplished gardener, Neptune acquired his
distinctive name as a result of having been
born in a rowboat on the way to the midwife
on neighbouring Mayne Island some ninety
years ago.

Opposite: Looking like wrought ironwork, the
sinuous intertwining forms of arbutus trees on
Pender Island are silhouetted against the sunset.

Opposite: Surrounded by their animals —
which also include several goats, numerous
chickens, and two beautiful horses — Ivan
and Brunie Naus live on Pender Island,
British Columbia.

Above: Richard Royal, here with his daughter
Tannis, raises hogs and sheep on Saltspring
Island, British Columbia, where some of the
best spring lamb in the world is produced.

Above: A log dumping and sorting area off the shore of Saltspring Island, British Columbia, viewed from the clifftop of Mount Maxwell.

Opposite: Quick to build in a region where timber is abundant, a split-rail fence marks the boundary of a sheep farm on Saltspring Island.

Above: Broken by the thaw and shunted about by winds and currents, sculptured slabs of pack ice jam the shore of Baffin Island along Pangnirtung Fiord off Cumberland Sound.

Opposite: Clearing weather reveals the unexpectedly tall mountains of Baffin Island, the most precipitous in Canada.

Overleaf: Inuit children play amidst grounded ice floes late on an August evening at Pangnirtung, Baffin Island.

Above: Broad-leaved willow herb and drifting
sand (often underlain by ice) form delicate
landscapes in the rocky Arctic valleys of
Baffin Island.

Opposite: A brook flowing down to the Weasel
River on Baffin Island rides over a plush
carpet of moss, starving it of oxygen and
turning it red.

''The Land That Never Melts,'' Auyuittuq
National Park on Baffin Island is dominated
by ice, rock, and clouds.

Suffused with the prolonged glow of the
gradual Arctic sunset, a mountain in
Auyuittuq National Park lies reflected in a
pool ringed with broad-leaved willow herb.

Above: The Rockview Trail is part of a
network of secluded footpaths on Beausoleil
Island, the largest of several dozen in Georgian
Bay Islands National Park, Ontario.

Opposite: A floating tapestry of pine needles
and maple leaves lies by a trailside in the
woods of Beausoleil Island.

Opposite: A weir for trapping perch, pickerel, bass, and whitefish stretches out from the shore of Pelee Island in Lake Erie. Hen Island sits on the horizon.

Above: Dealing mostly in quality ceramics and woollens, Elmer F. Holl of Pelee Island operates the southernmost store in Canada.

Opposite: Sculpting rows of snowdrifts, bitter
winds knife across the farm fields of Île
d'Orléans above Québec City.

Above: Rows of harvested peat stand
illuminated in the afternoon sun on Île aux
Coudres in the St. Lawrence River, Québec.

Above: Joe Myers, with Herb Leavitt in the
background, turns a block of distinctively
grained bird's-eye maple in the workshop of
Leavitt's Maple Tree Craft in Alberton,
Prince Edward Island.

Opposite: The low evening sun accentuates
the pattern of wind-rippled sand on Stanhope
Beach in Prince Edward Island National Park.

Opposite: Dusk settles around a small church
at Glenwood in Prince County,
Prince Edward Island.

Above: Employing several skilled artisans, the
Toy Factory at Murray River, Prince Edward
Island, produces numerous wooden toys and
other hand-crafted items.

Rapidly eroding red sandstone cliffs,
such as this headland at Grande Entrée, are
common in Québec's Magdalen Islands.

A lone farmhouse under a darkening sky near
Leslie on Grosse Île in the Magdalen Islands.

Opposite upper: Clouds brood over the
cemetery at La Vernière on the island of Cap
aux Meules in the Magdalens.

Opposite lower: The church of Saint-Pierre at
La Vernière, Magdalen Islands.

Above: The shoreline of the Magdalen Islands
consists of very long sandy beaches framed
between sections of soft red rock, as in this
scene at Old Harry.

Above: Sundown at Campobello, New Brunswick; the tide rushes in, cutting the Sugar Loaf Rocks off from Liberty Point.

Opposite: Fishermen's shanties lie mirrored behind the breakwater at Seal Cove, Grand Manan Island, New Brunswick.

Opposite: The drama of the sea is manifest near Westport, Brier Island, where Joshua Slocum, the first man to sail alone around the world, was raised.

Above: Centuries of incoming and outgoing tides have rolled angular chunks of basalt into a pavement of smoothly rounded stones on Brier Island, Nova Scotia.

Above: Lobster pots on Morris Island in
southern Nova Scotia lie stacked, ready for
the winter season.

Opposite: Nets and floats on Cape Sable
Island, one of Nova Scotia's main ocean
fishing centres and famous for the building of
Cape Island boats.

Opposite: A sprinkling of snow and the golden light of a low winter sun enhance the rugged beauty of the shore of Cape Breton Highlands National Park.

Above: The silent work of fresh snow puts the icing on this platinum-pure scene at North River, Cape Breton Island.

Opposite: Capped with several thousand nesting gannets and separated from the main shore by a sheer-walled gap, Bird Rock looms through the mists at Cape St. Mary's, Newfoundland.

Above: The roar of majestic surf at the base of hundred-metre-high cliffs mingles with the cries of tens of thousands of sea birds at Cape St. Mary's.

Opposite: Magnificent birds with a two-metre
wing span, gannets spend their first three
years entirely at sea, after which they return
to their place of birth to breed.

Above: Kittiwakes nest on tiny ledges on the
face of sheer cliffs. The young, readily
identifiable by the black markings on their
wings, are especially elegant.

Overleaf: A catch of cod is unloaded on a July
evening at Island Harbour, Fogo Island,
Newfoundland. Change Island spans
the horizon.

Boats and buttercups preoccupy children
on Fogo Island.

Ranks of gravestones overlook Notre Dame
Bay at Twillingate, the main community on
Newfoundland's Twillingate Island.

Above: The result of a few handfuls of seed
casually tossed on the ground, lupins spill out
of a yard on Bell Island, Newfoundland.

Opposite: The ruins left behind by iron mining
are everywhere on Bell Island; the fishing
goes on, as it always has.

Opposite: Fishermen's shacks crowd the shore
at lower Lance Cove on Random Island,
Newfoundland.

Above: Freshly painted boats lie bottoms-up in
a builder's yard at Gander Bay,
Newfoundland.

The lighthouse at Cape Spear, Newfoundland,
marks the easternmost point in North America.

Index

Anticosti Island, 40-41
Baffin Island, 9, 86-93
Balaklava Island, 66-67
Beausoleil Island, 94-95
Bell Island, 124-25
Bird Rock, 116
Bird sanctuary islands, 50, 116
Brier Island, 1, 7, 110-11
Campobello Island, 108
Cap aux Meules, 106
Cape Breton Island, 48, 114-15
Cape Sable Island, 14, 113
Cormorant Island, 63
Coudres, Île aux, 39, 99
Demoiselle, Île de la, 49
Fishing Islands, 30
Fogo Island, 51-53, 120-22
Galiano Island, 74-75, 77-79
Georgian Bay islands, 28-29, 94-95
Grande Entrée, 104
Grand Manan Island, 109
Great Lakes islands, 6, 25-33, 94-97
Grosse Île (Magdalens), 105
Grosse Île (St. Lawrence River), 38

Gulf Islands, 4, 10, 14, 16, 22-24, 70-85
Hornby Island, 69, 71
Inside Passage, 21
Long Island (Nova Scotia), 15
Magdalen Islands, 45-46, 104-107
Manitoulin Island, 28-29
Mayne Island, 70
Montréal islands, 35-36
Morris Island, 112
Newfoundland, 3, 8, 54-55, 116-27
Nova Scotian islands, 1, 7, 14, 15,
    47, 110-15
Orléans, Île de, 37, 98
Pelee Island, 31-32, 96-97
Pender Island, 4, 10, 81-82
Porcher Island, 64
Prince Edward Island, 42-44, 100-103
Quadra Island, 68
Queen Charlotte Islands, 17-20, 57-62
Random Island, 126
St. Joseph Island, 6, 26-27
Saltspring Island, 14, 16, 83-85
Texada Island, 65
Thousand Islands, 34
Toronto Islands, 33
Twillingate Island, 123
Vancouver Island, 2

Editor/Carlotta Lemieux
Design/David Shaw & Associates Ltd.
Composition/Attic Typesetting
Colour separation/Artcraft Engravers Ltd.
Manufacture/The Bryant Press Ltd.